"Jane Dalton, Elizabeth Hope Dorman, and Kathryn Byrnes are to be commended for this vitally required three-volume series for the field of contemplative teacher education. At a time where, on a global scale, radical changes in K–12 curricula are occurring, these volumes are indeed welcome. Doubling down on instructional strategies, e-learning devices, and content expertise miss the point entirely: we need to attend to the inner lives of aspiring teachers so they in turn can foster a learning environment that honors both the interior and exterior world of students." —**Heesoon Bai, Laurie Anderson, and Charles Scott**, program coordinators of Master of Education in Contemplative Inquiry and Approaches to Education, Simon Fraser University, Canada

"This book is a well-timed intervention in a historical moment in which disinformation can be proliferated as swiftly information, making the task of distinguishing truth from falsehood more difficult. The ability to discriminate truth from lies, wise from rash action and a predisposition to choose the former rather than the latter is the core of teaching. It requires more than logical analysis and reason can provide. Far from being practices of social disengagement, contemplative practices are more varied, scientific, and socially significant than conventional education has admitted; our need for them in education could not be greater." —**David Gall**, associate professor, art education, University of North Carolina at Charlotte, author of *Countering Modernity: Toward a Non-dualist Basis for Art Education*

"In *The Teaching Self*, authors provide tools for connecting their professional lives as teachers to their inner lives through contemplative practices. These practices bring forth a whole person, an authentic, loving teacher who is fully 'present' while educating today's students. This wholeness represents balance between the rational/analytical and the intuitive/emotional aspects of the teacher. This research is timely and relevant in our current, hurried world." —**Laurel H. Campbell**, Ed.D, Purdue University Fort Wayne, co-editor of *The Heart of Art Education: Holistic Approaches to Creativity, Integration, and Transformation*

"In an age where education is increasingly dominated by extrinsic forces (standards, accountability, etc.), this volume of thought-provoking essays offers an important counterpoint: the need for teachers to attend to their own intrinsic development as well as that of their students. Under the broad heading of contemplative pedagogy, the book addresses teachers in diverse contexts with a range of topics, including: cultural responsiveness in preservice teacher education, integrating the arts for personal transformation, developing empathy and authenticity, and the teacher's path to mindfulness. The book is a welcome addition to the literature on holistic education and reflective practice in schools." —**Seymour Simmons III**, Ed.D., professor of Fine Arts emeritus, Winthrop University, coeditor, *The Heart of Art Education: Holistic Approaches to Creativity, Integration, and Transformation*

"*The Teaching Self: Contemplative Practices, Pedagogy, and Research in Education* is a profound and crucial wake-up call in the field of education. A collection of brilliant insights—contemporary and historical—into the need for mind-body-spirit balance and how to accomplish that in today's varied teaching environments. These educators value 'process over product,' a real coup in a world that needs more authenticity. This is precisely the sort of revamping our educational systems need!" —**Chris Saade**, author of *Second Wave Spirituality: Passion for Peace, Passion for Justice*

The Teaching Self

The Teaching Self

Contemplative Practices, Pedagogy, and Research in Education

Edited by
Jane E. Dalton,
Elizabeth Hope Dorman,
and
Kathryn Byrnes

ROWMAN & LITTLEFIELD
Lanham • Boulder • New York • London

Published by Rowman & Littlefield
A wholly owned subsidiary of The Rowman & Littlefield Publishing Group, Inc.
4501 Forbes Boulevard, Suite 200, Lanham, Maryland 20706
www.rowman.com

Unit A, Whitacre Mews, 26-34 Stannary Street, London SE11 4AB

British Library Cataloguing in Publication Information Available

Library of Congress Cataloging-in-Publication Data Available

ISBN 978-1-4758-3631-8 (cloth : alk. paper)
ISBN 978-1-4758-3632-5 (pbk. : alk. paper)
ISBN 978-1-4758-3633-2 (electronic)

♾ ™ The paper used in this publication meets the minimum requirements of American National Standard for Information Sciences Permanence of Paper for Printed Library Materials, ANSI/NISO Z39.48-1992.

Printed in the United States of America

Contents

Foreword

Laura I. Rendón

It never fails. When I address educators and ask them to identify the one or two key competencies that are absolutely essential for students to learn when they graduate from college, we generate two lists, depicting both intellectual and inner aptitudes. The longest competency list that emerges relates to inner-life skills; for example, being authentic, having integrity, working well with others, having a sense of meaning and purpose, seeing the glass half full, practicing presence, developing wisdom, having self-awareness, practicing empathy, seeking justice, and being open to new ideas. And when I follow up and ask them how much time they spend developing exactly what they consider to be the most important competencies students should have learned when they leave college, there is an awkward silence and sometimes nervous laughter as educators realize that most of what they have done is to focus on traditional measures of learning related to cognitive development.

This simple exercise exemplifies that we are out of balance in education, and it is time to address this imbalance with a newly fashioned paradigm that appreciates and fosters not only intellectual development, but also abilities that allow an individual to access inner knowing related to emotions, intuition, and wisdom. Not only are we out of balance, but this is a challenging, complex time when the demands of the teaching profession have become quite overwhelming, necessitating a new perspective that focuses on what and how to teach, as well as on the teacher whose role it is to construct and facilitate a pedagogy of wholeness. There is little professional development training for teachers to work with a pedagogy of wholeness which includes contemplative practices.

To that end, Jane E. Dalton, Elizabeth Hope Dorman, and Kathryn Byrnes have edited a collective trio of books providing invigorating, innovative ways that contemplative pedagogy can deepen the work of teaching and learning in today's P–12 classrooms. What the authors theorize is that contemplative pedagogy that focuses on deep learning experiences and reflective practices can strengthen teaching and learning, while supporting and enhancing teacher development. As suggested by Hawkins' (2007) framing of I, Thou, and It as the central relationships in the teaching and learning process, each of the three books complement each other and are arranged to cover three important aspects of meaningful learning experiences as follows.

The first book, *Cultivating A Culture of Learning: Contemplative Practices, Pedagogy, and Research in Education*, attends to the *content of teaching (It)*, with concrete examples of how to integrate contemplative practices in teacher education courses and programs.

The second book, *Impacting Teaching and Learning: Contemplative Practices, Pedagogy, and Research in Education*, addresses the *who that is being taught (Thou)*, and features current research on the impacts of contemplative practices and pedagogy in teacher education.

The third book, *The Teaching Self: Contemplative Practices, Pedagogy, and Research in Education*, focuses on *who is doing the teaching (I)*, with a focus on the teaching self.

Collectively, these three books are representative of what I call Sentipensante (Sensing/Thinking) Pedagogy (Rendón, 2009, 2011). A sensing/thinking pedagogy disrupts the entrenched notion that education should focus mainly, if not solely, on developing intellectual abilities such as critical thinking and problem solving. As in sentipensante pedagogy, a more spacious view of education is offered in these three books, one that connects and places into balance outer knowing (intellectual reasoning, rationality, and objectivity) with inner knowing (deep wisdom, sense of wonder, introspection, and emotion). The books stress the development of the whole person, and that educators should attend to all facets of our humanity—intellectual, social, emotional, and spiritual. In these books is the most cutting-edge information about contemplative pedagogy and its relationship to teacher education, including its uses, its challenges, and its promise. Epistemologically, these books move away from over-privileging Rene Descartes's "I think therefore I am," and toward modeling Audre Lorde's "I feel, therefore I can be free" (1984, p. 100). The authors get it right. Quite simply, education is not just about the mind; it is also about our emotions and about our social and spiritual development.

In Book III, the authors collectively accentuate that teacher educators, as well as preservice candidates who seek to engage a contemplative path, need to turn their attention to the "teaching self," an exquisite inward journey focusing on personal awareness, learning from triumphs and downfalls, coming to terms with personal shadows, and opening one's self to vulnerability and personal transformation. What happens in our hearts and minds plays out in our relationship with others and with the world at large. In some ways this is a radical personal professional development path. Too often traditional educators tend to view contemplative tools and practices as too "touchy feely," leading some to fear even sharing that they are working with a contemplative educational paradigm.

Breaking free from the traditional aspects of teaching and learning that do not serve us well takes courage. Contemplative educators learn by facing and conquering fear and by learning from the experience of inward observation, self-awareness, insight, compassion for others, and appreciation of the interconnectedness of life. Attention to the inner terrain can lead to informed judgment and wisdom in approaching difficult challenges with schooling and issues of social justice. This is an example of praxis; action based on personal reflection and growth and the reciprocal relationship between theory and practice.

A number of themes emerge from this volume focusing on the teaching self. The first relates to the journey of the contemplative educator, one that involves the importance of professional development in the uses of contemplative tools which could include attending workshops, meditation retreats, and conferences. Self-awareness and personal growth over time characterize some of these journeys as educators learn from both positive and negative life and schooling experiences.

A second theme is the acknowledgement that contemplative education has significant benefits and could be the missing link toward fostering true educational excellence in schools. The benefits include but are not limited to increased student overall well-being, improved academic performance, the humanization of education, authentic teaching and learning, and the fostering of healthy relationships between teachers and students.

Growing student diversity leads us to the third theme in this book, the relationship between contemplative education and culturally responsive teaching. The nation is witnessing a remarkable demographic transformation which is revealing itself in our educational system. Today, more than half of all children under age five are of color, and by 2044 people of color will comprise the majority population in the United States (http://nationalequity atlas.org/data-summaries). Related to this theme is the notion that many teachers, especially those from middle- and upper-class backgrounds, are typically not well prepared to work with students of color and many have not been exposed to communities of color. Regrettably, some teachers default to employing deficit-based perspectives about students, while harboring damaging biases and assumptions. Resistance, denial, push back, and White fragility (DiAngelo, 2011) preclude productive working relationships with students of color and their families.

The field of contemplative education has addressed in a limited fashion issues related to working with a culturally diverse student body. As Rendon & Kanagala (2014) note,

A newly fashioned imaginary of teaching and learning for diversity and social justice requires that faculty rethink the way they teach, select content material and classroom learning activities, engage with students, and foster reflective processes. This critical task has enormous potential and carries both risks and rewards. (p. 74)

This volume provides positive directions in contemplative education's important role to play in addressing culturally responsive teaching. This includes building trust, having compassion, and fostering the development of social-emotional skills.

At the same time, to be nonoppressive and nondiscriminatory, teacher educators and preservice teachers must address their own racial biases and stereotypical views with the assistance of inner life practices such as mindfulness and meditation and continued openness to individual learning and personal growth. Getting professional training, testing and retesting ideas, practicing compassion, developing empathy, embodying presence, and learning from successes and failures are helpful in creating one's own pedagogical toolbox. Teachable moments exist everywhere and no experience, however challenging, should be wasted.

A fourth theme in this third book relates to the diverse array of contemplative practices that teachers can learn to employ. This collection of book chapters offers readers well-known tools such as mindfulness, Social Emotional Learning (SEL), meditation, and journaling. The authors also discuss other contemplative practices, some of which may not be well known. These include breath work, connecting the arts with *Lectio Divina*, silence, Wait Time, deep listening, contemplative arts, pedagogical bricolage, contemplation of impermanence, sand mandalas, *pedamantras* (i.e. pedagogical mantras), and Stage Exercise.

This collection of three books plays an integral part in moving education to a new consciousness, one that challenges, if not shatters, hegemonic assumptions about teaching and learning, including the privileging of positivist assumptions about detachment and objectivity, Eurocentrism as the only credible way of knowing, the separation of teacher and student, and the separation of reason from emotion. What is being offered in these books is a politic of affinity and connectedness, and the ontological view that humanity at its core seeks relationships and a sense of belonging. Thinking and feeling share equal status and become, as Lorde expresses, "a choice of ways and explorations" (1984, p. 101) to seek knowledge and to form truths.

These three books should be required reading, especially for the new generation of students seeking to enter the teaching profession and who believe that values and ethical practices such as community, personal and social responsibility, integrity, truth-telling, and self-reflection must share an equal space with cognitive development in a school classroom. Of significant import is that these books represent a marvelous pedagogic gift from courageous educators who have dared to take risks, have followed their intuition about what an authentic classroom should be, and have stayed true to the original impulse that drove them into the teaching profession.

I imagine that if you have picked up any one of these three books that something inside of you is seeking something different, something authentic, something that speaks to the whole of your being. Look no more. In your hands are exemplars of authentic teacher training, holistic student development, and the cultivation of classrooms guided by rigorous intellectual pursuits and the foundation for building an educational system that aspires to democratic ideals, humanitarianism, culturally responsive practices, and the common good. In your hands is the foundation for the evolution of a new story of what it means to prepare educators to facilitate student learning in a world that is desperately calling for ethical leaders who can (with intelligence, insight and wisdom) deal with the contradictions, uncertainties, messiness and complications of our lives. I applaud this inspiring, groundbreaking work, and encourage you to become an integral part of shaping the new story of education based on wholeness and guided by the ultimate expression of our values—love.

Laura I. Rendón, author of *Sentipensante (Sensing/Thinking) Pedagogy: Educating for Wholeness, Social Justice and Liberation* (2009), Stylus Press

REFERENCES

DiAngelo, R. (2011). White fragility. *International Journal of Critical Pedagogy, 3*(3), 54–70.

Hawkins, D. (2007). *The informed vision: Essays on learning and human nature.* Algora Publishing.

Lorde, A. (1984). *Sister outsider: Essays and speeches.* Berkeley, CA: Crossing Press.

National Equity Atlas (n.d.). Data Summaries. http://nationalequityatlas.org/data-summaries.

Rendón, L. I. (2009). *Sentipensante (sensing/thinking) pedagogy: Educating for wholeness, social justice and liberation.* Sterling, VA: Stylus Press.

Rendón, L. I. (2011). Cultivating una persona educada. A sentipensante (sensing/thinking) vision of education. *Journal of College and Character, 12*(2), 1–9.

Rendón, L. I., & Kanagala, V. (2014). Embracing contemplative pedagogy in a culturally diverse classroom. In B. F. Tobolowsky (Ed.). *Paths to learning: Teaching for engagement in college* (pp. 61–76). Columbia, SC: University of South Carolina, National Resource Center for the First-Year Experience and Students in Transition.

Acknowledgments

This book has been inspired and nurtured by many educators, artists, scholars, and contemplatives. Our heartfelt gratitude to those educators, past and present, who have been instrumental in opening the contemplative path, and to the students whose search for meaning and purpose provided inspiration for and feedback during the journey.

We are grateful to all of those with whom we have had the pleasure to work during the development and publication of this series of books. Without the vision and dedication of the volume 3 authors—Deborah Ann Donahue-Keegan, Timothy E. Jester, David Lee Keiser, Jambay Lhamo, Matthew Spurlin, Katinka Gøtzsche, Elizabeth Grassi, and Heather Bair—this series would not be possible. Thank you.

Each unique voice and perspective offers a richly complex tapestry of ways to integrate contemplative practice, pedagogy, and research into the field of teacher education. We extend a special thanks to Tom Koerner, Carlie Wall, and Emily Tuttle at Rowman and Littlefield for their support during this process.

We are also especially grateful to Laura I. Rendón, professor emeritus at the University of Texas–San Antonio and author of *Sentipensante (Sensing/ Thinking) Pedagogy: Educating for Wholeness, Social Justice, and Liberation* for writing the profound, inspired forewords for each of the three volumes in this series.

We feel especially humbled by the collaboration, support, friendship, and collegiality that has developed over the years as we, the editors, worked together to develop, refine, and publish this book series. We are honored to curate such a meaningful, inspired, and inspiring series of books for future generations of teacher educators, educators, and students.

Jane E. Dalton
Elizabeth Hope Dorman
Kathryn Byrnes

Introduction

Jane E. Dalton, University of North Carolina at
Charlotte, Charlotte, North Carolina;
Elizabeth Hope Dorman, Fort Lewis College,
Durango, Colorado;
Kathryn Byrnes, Bowdoin College,
Brunswick, Maine

Cultivating a culture of learning in education demands courageous commitment and willingness to step into the unknown and model authentic engagement through compassionate, experiential, personal practice. Contemplative pedagogy cultivates self-awareness and intra- and interpersonal skills, and deepens learning through practices such as breath awareness, meditation, silence, *Lectio Divina*, and the arts. As with all emergent curriculum, timely discourse is needed to illuminate the multiple ways in which contemplative pedagogy strengthens teaching and learning in classrooms and supports teacher development.

Typically, teacher education dedicates significant time to building capacities learned from external authorities, with an overemphasis on tips, tricks, and techniques of the profession. Rubrics, assessments, instructional strategies, curriculum mapping, and classroom management all privilege rational and empirical knowing across disciplines. Yet if educators are prepared to rely solely on external authorities as a gauge for pedagogical decisions, they fail to develop their full capacities, limiting their effectiveness.

Teaching and learning, at its best, is one of the most elemental of human exchanges and requires that we take responsibility for what, how, and why we teach, and who we are as teachers. Hawkins (2007) suggests that meaningful learning experiences rely on three interdependent facets: "It"—the content of teaching; "Thou"—who is being taught; and "I"—who is teaching.

Opening the door to contemplation in teacher education facilitates teacher reflection that deepens content knowledge, relationships with students, and self-awareness of the I as teacher.

Teaching demands we engage all dimensions of human awareness and action. As critical practitioners of the human experience, educators navigate several worlds—the inner realm of one's personal life and the outer worlds of his or her classroom, students, and school. As Palmer (1997) observes, "External tools of power have occasional utility in teaching, but they are no substitute for the authority that comes from the teacher's inner life. The clue is in the word itself, which has 'author' at its core" (p. 19).

Educators become the authors of their lives and access the inner life—through first-person contemplative experience, second-person dialogue and reflection in community, and third-person narratives of inspiration and guidance—through the integration of contemplative theory, research, and practice in teacher education. The overwhelmingly positive response to our call for chapter submissions demonstrated an interest in the ways in which contemplative practices, pedagogy, and research are being integrated into teacher education globally.

We have organized this scholarship within the field of contemplative teacher education into three books that address the following themes: *Cultivating a Culture of Learning, Impacting Teaching and Learning,* and *The Teaching Self.* Together these books offer varying insights into the multiple ways that contemplative theory, practices, and research appear in teacher education. In each book, critical global perspectives address the challenges of implementation along with the benefits of contemplative practices and pedagogy.

The first book focuses on the "It," the integration of contemplative practices in teacher education courses and programs, which is often the most salient and pragmatic approach for teacher educators. The second book addresses the "Thou," current research on the impacts of contemplative practices and pedagogy in teacher education. The third book returns our attention to the teaching self, the "Who." It is our hope that these three volumes will contribute to the ongoing dialogue about contemplative pedagogy in teacher education.

The final book in this series, *The Teaching Self: Contemplative Practices, Pedagogy, and Research in Education,* is a rich collection of voices from diverse settings that illustrates the ways in which first-person experiences with contemplative practices lay a foundation for contemplative pedagogy and research in teacher education. Contemplative practice depends on cultivating an understanding of oneself as well as one's relationship to and interdependence with others and the world. It is this precept that guides the focus of these reflective portraits.

The teaching self of the scholar benefits from reflective and authentic engagement and a commitment to equity and ethical action. Several authors examine the direct and indirect influence contemplative practices have on their students as future educators. The contributors in this book share first-hand experiences with contemplative practices that honor, support, and deepen awareness of the teaching self by exploring the journey of identifying as a contemplative educator.

The following paragraphs offer highlights of each of the eight chapters in this book.

Chapter 1, "Cultivating Culturally Responsive Teaching in Teacher Preparation: The Vital Role of Contemplative Teacher Educators," by Deborah Ann Donahue-Keegan, demonstrates how teacher educators committed to fostering culturally responsive practices in their work with preservice candidates are called to develop awareness of and critically reflect on their own held biases and assumptions. Based on interviews with six teacher educators as part of a small-scale pilot study, this chapter explores how contemplative practices may support teacher educators' efforts to cultivate culturally responsive teaching skills among preservice candidates.

Chapter 2, "Embracing a Contemplative Life: Art and Teaching as a Journey of Transformation," by Jane E. Dalton, explores including the arts in conjunction with *Lectio Divina* as a contemplative practice to facilitate personal transformation. The arts are deeply embedded with senses and mind-body action and reaction, a knowing and feeling that includes more of the expansive range of human experience and offers insight and awareness. These transformative experiences quiet the mind, awaken creativity, and deepen awareness by expanding emotional depth that allows for the knowing of the self through words and symbols.

Chapter 3, "Considering the Self Who Teaches," by Timothy E. Jester, discusses significant changes in the author's perspective about the purpose of schooling and his role as a teacher educator working for social justice. Underlying and supporting these transformative learning experiences has been a deepening in mindful awareness, compassion, and wholeness cultivated through the contemplative practices of sitting meditation and journaling.

Chapter 4, "If We Teach Who We Are, Who Are We? Mining the Self for More Mindful Teaching," by David Lee Keiser, speaks to the challenge of both maintaining a contemplative presence with preservice teachers and challenging them to be open to new experiences. He introduces the concept of pedagogical bricolage, challenging himself as well as his students to use all experiences as materials for one's teaching toolbox. He also presents other specific exercises used with preservice teachers to help them develop authentic teaching presence and identity.

Chapter 5, "Contemplative Wait Time: Pausing to Cultivate Compassion in the Classroom," by Jambay Lhamo, explores how contemplative wait time and the more generalized practice of pausing in the classroom nurture a safe and healthy learning environment through compassion. Pausing deepens self-awareness, which facilitates mindful speaking, deep listening, and embodied presence while teaching. The practice of wait time as a contemplative pedagogical practice nurtures increased awareness of one's own teaching behavior by being fully present with the students. The increased awareness encourages empathy with the students' situations without being judgmental.

Chapter 6, "Sustainability through Authenticity: A Portrait of Teaching as a Contemplative Practice," by Matthew Spurlin, focuses on the specific ways in which a contemplative teacher educator with more than 40 years in the field utilizes the perspective of *teaching as a contemplative practice* to recognize his authentic self in teaching, which demonstrably leads to sustainability—longevity—within the profession.

Chapter 7, "Building Relational Competence by Training Empathy," by Katinka Gøtzsche, describes the five natural competencies all human beings are born with: the ability to sense the body on different levels, the ability to breathe, the ability to sense feeling from the heart and attach to other people, the ability to be creative in the manner of adapting and reacting on impulses, and the ability to be awake and aware. The chapter describes a project intended to increase awareness of these natural competencies in both a contemplative and a dialogical manner as a way to strengthen and build teachers' relational competence.

Chapter 8, "Community, Compassion, and Embodying Presence in Contemplative Teacher Education," by Elizabeth Grassi and Heather Bair, describes the experience of one teacher educator who, early in her career, prepared teachers by integrating community involvement and reflection into the curriculum, and later evolved to understand the importance of compassion, embodying presence, and a contemplative approach to teacher education. This chapter provides examples of how this journey impacted her identity as a teacher educator as well as practices for preparing preservice teachers.

REFERENCES

Hawkins, D. (2007). *The informed vision: Essays on learning and human nature.* New York: Algora Publishing.

Palmer, P. J. (1997, November 1). The heart of a teacher: Identity and integrity in teaching. *Change: The Magazine of Higher Learning, 29*(6), 14–21.

Chapter One

Cultivating Culturally Responsive Teaching in Teacher Preparation

The Vital Role of Contemplative Teacher Educators

Deborah Ann Donahue-Keegan, Tufts University, Medford, Massachusetts

> Helping student teachers negotiate the zig and zag of their emotions, contend with the emotional lives of their students, and understand how what is happening inside of them shapes how they teach and how their own students perceive them is a critical element of supporting our new teachers. (Intrator, 2006, p. 234)

To truly support preservice teachers in the ways Intrator (2006) describes, teacher educators are also called to negotiate the "zig and zag" of their own emotional lives. This is particularly true for teacher educators who are committed to culturally responsive teaching and aim to prepare preservice candidates to address competently the complex equity issues and challenges that come with teaching in US public schools. The majority of teachers in K–12 schools work with students from racial, cultural, linguistic, and/or socioeconomic backgrounds very different from their own (US Department of Education, 2016). This documented "diversity gap" is projected to continue, and widen, in the coming decades (Putnam, Hansen, Walsh, & Quintero, 2016).

Villegas and Lucas (2002) have long argued that that teacher preparation programs, and teacher educators more specifically, need to move beyond a "fragmented and superficial treatment of diversity" (p. 20) toward advancing strength-based teaching practices and disrupting the pervasive deficit thinking paradigm entrenched in many school systems (Valencia, 2010; Weiner, 2006). Yet McKenzie and Phillips's recent (2016) study of equity consciousness among new teachers reveals that novice teachers are still too often "caught in equity traps" marked by deficit views, racial erasure thinking, and blind acceptance of meritocracy.

Guiding preservice teachers to develop racial literacy and cultural competence for their work with students in a racialized society and education system is complex and emotionally intensive; it is a process that must go beyond merely promoting cultural sensitivity (Stevenson, 2013). For teacher educators committed to culturally responsive practices, this process inevitably calls them to face and reflect upon their own held biases, assumptions, and cultural misattributions. It also involves navigating emotionally laden tensions in their efforts to facilitate dialogue and address issues regarding identity and social location.

Given the complex social-emotional and ethical dimensions of this work, how might contemplative practices support teacher educators' efforts to cultivate culturally responsive teaching skills among preservice candidates? Guided by this inquiry, this chapter centers on the following questions: In what ways, if any, do teacher educators with a demonstrated commitment to both mindfulness and culturally responsive teaching incorporate contemplative practices into their work with preservice teachers? What are the challenges, possibilities, and insights they describe?

To explore these questions, one-on-one initial interviews were conducted with six teacher educators to establish a baseline of perspectives as a springboard to further inquiry. All interviewees (each assigned a pseudonym for the purposes of this chapter) identify as contemplative practitioners; all but one participated in at least one of the following intensive mindfulness-focused professional development programs for educators: the Greater Good Science Center's Summer Institute for Educators and/or the Cultivating Awareness and Resiliency for Educators (CARE) Summer Institute.

The teacher educators interviewed for this small-scale study work in a range of teacher preparation programs. One is on the faculty of an urban residency program; the other five work with preservice teachers in different types of higher education programs (from university to community college levels, in both urban and suburban settings).

This chapter draws on and presents an overview of insights garnered through conversations with these contemplative teacher educators, all of whom identify as female. Two study participants identify as Black, one as an Arab American person of color, and the three others as White. A sampling of their compelling narrative accounts is included to capture key themes across interviews.

RACIAL/CULTURAL TENSIONS IN TEACHER PREPARATION

All the teacher educators interviewed described the varying ways in which they have experienced and learned from racial/cultural dissonance within their respective teacher preparation programs. This dissonance has been experienced both systemically, within institutional and program structures, as well as interpersonally. For the purpose of this chapter, the focus is on their experience of this dissonance in relationship to/with the preservice candidates they teach and mentor. In this section, the experiences of two interviewees, Deanna and La'Shanda, are highlighted.

Deanna is a White teacher educator who has worked with undergraduate preservice teachers in a teacher education program within a highly competitive university over the past 11 years. During her interview for this chapter, Deanna recounted a "stressful, humbling situation" she had experienced during her first year as a teacher educator in this program. This "situation" involved her efforts to address racism in an intensive summer course titled Diversity Awareness in Schools:

> I was completely in over my head in my attempts to constructively lead this group of seventeen students to examine their privileges, or lack thereof, and the ways they were complicit in a system marked by racism. Fourteen of these students were White, and mostly female, while three were African American, one female and two males. . . .
>
> My preparation for this was way too thin. The main problem was that I hadn't yet done the inner work I needed to do. I thought using a problem-posing approach à la Freire would get us to do some productive, important work as a group, and individually. . . .
>
> I was completely thrown off by the level of resistance, denial, and pushback among most of the White students, and by the intensity of the anger expressed by the few Black students, mostly in response to White students' resistance and, frankly, ignorant statements and accusations.
>
> Several White students within the group were very emotionally reactive and hostile; they expressed frustration that we weren't focusing on the nitty-gritty "how to" of classroom teaching. I ended up feeling personally attacked by the backlash, and so confused about what to do. How we finished this course is kind of a blur for me. What is clear is that this experience was the opposite of what I had intended it to be. (Deanna, personal communication)

What Deanna describes is an experience that is an all-too-common phenomenon for teacher educators who intentionally address both structural and individual (intra- and interpersonal) dimensions of institutional racism in their work with preservice candidates. It is a complicated, tension-filled, and emotionally laden process in numerous and varying ways.

Among the myriad themes touched upon in Deanna's description, one that also stands out across interviews for this chapter involves what all interviewees described as White preserve teachers' defensive resistance to reflecting on and talking about the intra- and interpersonal dimensions of institutional racism, specifically in terms of White privilege. This phenomenon points to what DiAngelo (2011) terms *White Fragility*,

> A state in which even a minimum amount of racial stress becomes intolerable, triggering a range of defensive moves. These moves include the outward display of emotions such as anger, fear, and guilt, and behaviors such as argumentation, silence, and leaving the stress-inducing situation. These behaviors, in turn, function to reinstate white racial equilibrium. (p. 54)

Similar White Fragility tensions were also described by La'Shanda, an interviewee who identifies as Black and teaches in an urban community college teacher preparation program. Like Deanna, La'Shanda described palpable racial stress tensions in her work with preservice candidates. She explained that because "many of [her] students struggle with mental health challenges," the "zig and zag" of social-emotional vulnerabilities tend to compound White Fragility tensions that inevitably arise when they address difficult issues around race, privilege, and social location.

La'Shanda described several situations when White preservice candidates in her classes "personalized issues, and turned their anger and frustrations on [her]." In La'Shanda's experience, directly addressing White Fragility within her teacher preparation courses is an emotionally draining process.

For teacher educators committed to guiding preservice candidates through this process, called for is ongoing development and expansion of their own conceptual and social-emotional repertoires, particularly because of the inevitable range of racial/cultural backgrounds, experiences, and awareness levels among their preservice students. Engaging deeply in this work inevitably involves reciprocal, interconnected, and developmentally spiraled learning, both for teacher educators and for their preservice students.

In their book *Talking Diversity with Teachers and Teacher Educators*, Cruz, Ellerbrock, Vásquez, and Howes (2014) identify five developmental stages preservice teachers tend to go through, to varying degrees, during the process of developing "diversity awareness" and a more evolved sense of their own identities: (1) naïveté/pre-awareness; (2) bombardment; (3) dissonance and resistance; (4) adjustment and redefinition; and (5) acceptance and internalization (p. 17). Proceeding through these stages involves intra- and interpersonal work that inevitably generates difficult emotions and learning for preservice candidates and teacher educators in differing ways.

To move through and beyond the "dissonance and resistance" stage, it is imperative for teacher educators to cultivate and maintain a baseline of relational trust. Otherwise, groups tend to get mired in this stage, often tinged with a palpable sense of anger, blaming, and shaming, as well as heightened denial and defensiveness. This is what unfolded within Deanna's group of preservice teachers as she stumblingly attempted to facilitate difficult dialogues around intersecting structural and individual levels of oppression and privilege. Her well-intentioned efforts as facilitator might have done more harm than good.

In different ways, both Deanna and La'Shanda conveyed their similar belief in the vital importance of establishing relational trust as well as their understanding that this process demands deepened awareness, learning, and skills on the part of teacher educators. Of the "stressful and humbling" situation Deanna described, she acknowledged that it was "a painful learning experience that [she] was reeling from for at least a year" (Deanna, personal communication).

Yet through deep self-reflection over time, she has come to see how this experience became a catalyst for transformative personal and professional learning. Reflecting on the layered dynamics of the situation, including her own mind-set and behaviors, has helped her to develop expanded conceptual and social-emotional repertoires, to more competently navigate the inevitable dissonances and dilemmas that come with culturally responsive teaching in an ethnically diverse and racialized society.

For La'Shanda, the difficult teaching situations she described are not only "very tricky to navigate as a person of color" but also emotionally triggering. Yet since incorporating mindfulness practice in her daily life over the past few years, La'Shanda reported that she "feels much better equipped" to navigate difficult racial-stress-related interactions by "facilitating the development of a climate of relational trust with students at the beginning of a semester" (La'Shanda, personal communication).

La'Shanda explained, "The biggest shift has been my focus on compassion, shifting from judgmental to nonjudgmental perspectives in relating with myself and with students; it's been life changing personally and professionally for me" (La'Shanda, personal communication). La'Shanda attributed this "life-changing" shift to her daily mindfulness practice.

SOCIAL-EMOTIONAL COMPETENCE AND STAMINA: WHAT'S MINDFULNESS GOT TO DO WITH IT?

In her book *Culturally Responsive Teaching and the Brain*, Hammond (2015) argues that authentic culturally responsive teaching is fundamentally about "being in relationship and having a social-emotional connection" (p. 15). She also emphasizes how and why it is vital for educators to continually develop and strengthen skills to constructively address "the social-emotional impact of living in a racialized society" (Hammond, cited in Malarkey,

2015)—that doing so is the cornerstone of authentic culturally responsive teaching:

> It's about recognizing the social-emotional impact of living in a racialized society where some people have unearned privilege and others have unearned disadvantage. Sometimes this is hard for teachers to address in a meaningful way that doesn't make them or students feel awkward. But it must be acknowledged. Unacknowledged implicit bias and racial stress have a negative impact on culturally and linguistically diverse students. It erodes their trust in us. . . .
>
> We have to first give teachers the tools to engage in conversations about racialization, which is different from racism. . . . They [often] don't have the social-emotional stamina to manage their fight-or-flight response when looking at social inequities. (Hammond, cited in Malarkey, 2015)

Social-emotional stamina hinges on social-emotional competence, which involves the ongoing development of the social-emotional learning (SEL) skills needed to recognize and manage emotions, handle conflict constructively, establish positive relationships guided by empathy, engage in perspective taking, make responsible decisions, and handle challenging situations effectively (Weissberg, Durlak, Domitrovich, & Gullotta, 2015). Social-emotional stamina is cultivated when an individual can consistently access and activate, as modus operandi, SEL skills across a broad range of situations, from no- to low-stress to highly stressful, complex, and contentious situations.

Social-emotional stamina is established and actualized when an individual develops a balanced, calm autonomic nervous system as a baseline state to manage fight-or-flight responses (Seppälä, 2016; Yuan & Silberstein, 2016). As confirmed by cutting-edge affective neuroscience research, such mindbody emotional balance can be better attained through strengthening one's vagus nerve, a neural network that extends from brain to gut; it is considered "a key nexus of mind and body and a biological building block of human compassion" (Keltner, 2012).

When a person develops social-emotional stamina, they are better able to access and activate social-emotional skills, compassion, and empathy during highly stressful personal and/or professional situations (Hammond, personal communication). Consistent, intentional breathing practices promote the development of social-emotional stamina and well-being through mindfulness, the practice of maintaining present-moment awareness and nonjudgmental acceptance of one's feelings, thoughts, and bodily sensations within the surround of one's environment (Greater Good Science Center, n.d.; Seppälä, 2016).

Research demonstrates how and why sustained mindfulness practices can lead to a simultaneous decrease in bodily stress hormones (e.g., cortisol) and increase in levels of dopamine and serotonin—neurotransmitters that promote emotion regulation and proactive relationship behaviors—and oxyto-cin, the hormone in service of positive relational connecting (Keltner, 2012).

Across individual interview conversations with the six teacher educators, each focused first and foremost on the vital role of mindfulness as an on-ramp to a greater sense of equanimity in their work to cultivate racial literacy and cultural competence among preservice teachers. In terms of the specific ways in which each of these teacher educators named benefits of mindful-ness, the following composite themes emerged. Interviewees reported that through consistent mindfulness practices, they had incorporated more of the following in their respective work with preservice teachers:

- listening more deeply and nonjudgmentally during classes and when ad-vising students in their respective school sites;
- responding rather than reacting to emotional distress that inevitably arises during classes;
- recognizing and managing strong emotions triggered during difficult di-alogues;
- examining their own assumptions and possible misinterpretations;
- being more receptive to learning about and from different perspectives;
- observing more calmly, clearly, and spaciously; and
- relating to their teacher preparation colleagues and students with greater sense of empathy and compassion.

DIFFICULT DIALOGUES, COMPASSIONATE LISTENING

Jasmin talked about how she continually struggles to strike a balance of support and challenge in working with preservice teachers in the urban teach-ing residency program within which she teaches. Jasmin, who identifies as an "Arab American person of color," talked at length about her commitment to cultivate introspection and transformational learning "around race, culture, and the oppressive education system that perpetuates social stratification and reproduction in society" (Jasmin, personal communication).

With a focus on building relational trust, cultivating compassion, and engaging in active listening, Jasmin works to create a "safe container" so that her students can develop the skills they need to constructively engage in critical reflection and difficult interactions. She explained:

> The majority of my students come from White middle-class backgrounds. The intersection piece continues to be hard for them. The reflection piece continues to be difficult for them. As a teacher, as the leader, I struggle with "What's my role? How do I do this? How do I support the conversation without it turning into a search for feeling good and comfortable again?"

But, doing it with compassion . . . but yet, holding the space for the conversation to happen. I do feel lucky that I go into the classroom, and observe them teach, and then I get to give them feedback, where we look at all of the discussions, and what it looks like in daily practice. So, one of the questions that they're now working on is "How are you giving Black and Brown students permission to not learn?" (Jasmin, personal communication)

Jasmin's reflections reveal the complex, nuanced dimensions involved in the developmental journey through the dissonance and resistance stages for most preservice teachers (Cruz et al., 2014). She echoed Hammond's observation that educators too often "do not have the social-emotional stamina to manage their fight-or-flight response" (Hammond, cited in Malarkey, 2015) while addressing social inequities, including their own implicit biases.

In her work with teacher candidates, Jasmin's integration of contemplative practices is more tacit than explicit. As the one interviewee who had not (yet) participated in intensive mindfulness-focused professional development programs for educators, Jasmin conveys that she focuses on her own intrapersonal reflection and mindfulness practices to nourish her as she works to create and maintain a "safe container" for new teachers she teaches and mentors.

Marian, a teacher educator on the East Coast, described ways her daily mindfulness practice helps her "become more compassionate, with a better capacity for listening" (Marian, personal communication). In recent years, she has intentionally and purposefully incorporated contemplative practices in her work with undergraduate preservice candidates (many of whom are White and from upper-income families) at a small private college in a suburban town.

Most of her students' practicum placements are in a nearby small city, in under-resourced schools serving culturally and linguistically diverse students (many from families living in poverty). Since explicitly integrating mindfulness practices in her preservice courses, Marian has noticed "a significant shift" in her preservice students' willingness "to engage in difficult dialogue regarding racial, class, religious and ethnic differences" (Marian, personal communication).

Like Marian, the other teacher educators interviewed for this chapter also credit mindfulness for better enabling them to foster interpersonal, intrapersonal, and intragroup receptivity (in their work with preservice candidates) in difficult dialogues regarding race, social location, and privilege. In myriad ways, they all talked about ways that mindfulness practices have helped them to be more present and better able to "negotiate the zig and zag of their emotions." They all conveyed in different ways what was stated by another interviewee, Aviva, who codirects a large, urban teacher preparation program: "Teacher educators need to put their oxygen masks on first," referencing Lantieri's 2009 article, "Putting the Oxygen Masks on Ourselves First."

Aviva also echoed other interviewees in her insightful reflections on what she views as vital to her role in the process of preparing preservice teachers:

> For me, it is really about the way that I am being with my students; it is a level of presence. I'm always teaching them about, and continually referring back to things like the iceberg, where there's one conversation happening above the surface, and then what's really happening underneath . . . and to be mindful of what's happening, and to listen for that in your interactions with your students.
>
> I do the same with my students. So, that's a practice that I do consistently, and that I recommend that they do consistently. I've found that that has a really deep impact on the level of relationships that people can have, and the level of connection that people can have. I encourage my students to teach and interact from that space. (Aviva, personal communication)

Aviva, who considers herself a "racially aware and literate" teacher educator, works closely with her colleagues to continually assess why, how, and to what extent they are helping teacher candidates develop culturally relevant, responsive, and contemplative practices. "The iceberg" is a metaphor to which she referred numerous times in describing how a contemplative approach influences her work as a teacher educator with a strong commitment to modeling and fostering social-emotionally attuned culturally responsive skills:

> I'm always really conscious about where the preservice teachers might be, how they might be listening, wherever they are in their own journey . . . and trying to be thoughtful in my approach, to help nurture their own growth. Whenever they do react, I try to be mindful of why they might be [reacting], and to gently guide their growth through questions, and through . . . connect[ing] with them wherever they might be. . . . And also, to be mindful of these same dynamics in their own classrooms.
>
> And then, oftentimes—to go back to the iceberg again—it is not necessarily that one of their students is doing something wrong; it's that culturally we might define it as wrong, as a White person. But maybe that student is just being expressive in their own cultural mannerisms, which may not really mean what [the preservice teacher] thinks they mean from [his or her own] White cultural lens.
>
> Again, it is still using that kind of way of looking and being that helps both my students and their growth, personally, in their journey, as well as the way that they see students that have various social identities that are different from theirs, that they are trying to understand . . . to continue to use that kind of approach to better understand. (Aviva, personal communication)

CONCLUSION

In a recent *Education Week* article, Sawchuk (2016) asserts that "merely emphasizing the tenets of culturally responsive pedagogy in coursework does not guarantee that aspiring teachers will be able to enact them in a classroom." Indeed, as described by the six teacher educators interviewed for this chapter, preparing preservice teachers for culturally responsive teaching is complicated and emotionally demanding. To model and cultivate authentic culturally responsive teaching skills in teacher preparation programs, teacher educators must first develop strong social-emotional stamina in order to reflect critically and authentically on their own held biases and assumptions.

All interviewees concomitantly conveyed, in varying ways, how their respective intrapersonal contemplative practices are vital to sustaining their efforts to cultivate culturally responsive social-emotional learning/development—both for themselves and in relationship with/to their preservice students. It is a process that involves transformative learning whereby educators engage in shifting their "frames of reference through critical reflection on the assumptions upon which [their] interpretations, beliefs, and habits of mind or points of view are based" (Mezirow, 1997, p. 7).

Developing racial literacy and cultural competence in teacher preparation programs is a relationally interconnected developmental endeavor for both teacher educators and preservice candidates. Reflective self-awareness and social-emotional stamina are the fulcrum of the process of developing authentic culturally responsive teaching practices that veer away from "equity traps" such as deficit thinking. Mindfulness is the on-ramp.

ESSENTIAL IDEAS TO CONSIDER

- Teacher educators committed to promoting culturally responsive social-emotional learning/development must first develop social-emotional stamina in order to reflect on their own held biases and assumptions before working with preservice candidates to address issues such as identity, social location, and intersectionality.
- Interviews conducted with six teacher educators revealed the different ways in which contemplative practices support teacher educators' efforts to model and foster authentic culturally responsive teaching skills in their work with preservice teachers.
- Interviewees described the myriad ways in which mindfulness is vital to their ongoing development of intrapersonal social-emotional stamina and helps them to practice greater equanimity in their work to cultivate culturally responsive social-emotional learning among preservice candidates in their respective teacher preparation programs.

REFERENCES

Cruz, B., Ellerbrock, C. R., Vásquez, A., & Howes, E. V. (Eds.). (2014). *Talking diversity with teachers and teacher educators: Exercises and critical conversations across the curriculum.* New York, NY: Teachers College Press.

DiAngelo, R. (2011). White fragility. *International Journal of Critical Pedagogy, 3*(3), 54–70. Retrieved from http://libjournal.uncg.edu/ijcp/article/view/249/116

Greater Good Science Center at University of California, Berkeley. (n.d.). Retrieved from http://greatergood.berkeley.edu/topic/mindfulness/definition

Hammond, Z. (2015). *Culturally responsive teaching and the brain: Promoting authentic engagement and rigor among culturally and linguistically diverse students.* Thousand Oaks, CA: Corwin.

Intrator, S. (2006). Beginning teachers and the emotional drama of the classroom. *Journal of Teacher Education, 30*(3), 271–289.

Keltner, D. (2012, July 31). The compassionate species. Greater Good Science Center at University of California, Berkeley. (n.d.). Retrieved from http://greatergood.berkeley.edu/article/item/the_compassionate_species

Lantieri, L. (2009, May). Putting the oxygen masks on ourselves first. *Reclaiming Youth International E-Newsletter.* Retrieved from http://www.innerresilience-tidescenter.org/publications.html

Malarkey, T. (2015, April 8). Culturally responsive teaching and the brain: An interview with Zaretta Hammond. The National Equity Project. Retrieved from https://www.youtube.com/watch?v=DzwobAYsDL4

McKenzie, K. B., & Phillips, G. A. (2016). Equity traps then and now: deficit thinking, racial erasure and naïve acceptance of meritocracy, *Whiteness and Education, 1*(1), 26–38. doi: 10.1080/23793406.2016.1159600

Mezirow, J. (1997). Transformative learning: Theory to practice. *New Directions for Adult and Continuing Education, 74*, 5–12. doi: 10.1002/ace.7401

Putnam, H., Hansen, M., Walsh, K., & Quintero, D. (2016). *High hopes and harsh realities: The real challenges to building a diverse workforce.* Brown Center on Education at Brookings. Retrieved from https://www.brookings.edu/research/high-hopes-and-harsh-realities-the-real-challenges-to-building-a-diverse-teacher-workforce/

Sawchuk, S. (2016, February 16). For preservice teachers, Lessons on cultural sensitivity. *Education Week.* Retrieved from http://www.edweek.org/ew/articles/2016/02/17/for-preservice-teachers-lessons-on-cultural-sensitivity.html

Seppälä, E. (2016). Breathing: The little-known secret to peace of mind. *Psychology Today.* Retrieved from https://emmaseppala.com/breathing-the-little-known-secret-to-peace-of-mind/

Stevenson, H. (2013). *Promoting racial literacy in schools: Differences that make a difference.* New York: Teachers College Press.

U.S. Department of Education, Office of Planning, Evaluation and Policy Development, Policy and Program Studies Service (2016). *The state of racial diversity in the educator workforce,* Washington, D.C. Retrieved from https://www2.ed.gov/rschstat/eval/highered/racial-diversity/state-racial-diversity-workforce.pdf

Valencia, R. (2010). *Dismantling contemporary deficit thinking: Educational thought and practice.* New York, NY: Routledge.

Villegas, A. M., & Lucas, T. (2002). Preparing culturally responsive teachers: Rethinking the curriculum. *Journal of Teacher Education, 53*(1), 20–32. doi: 10.1177/0022487102053001003

Weiner, L. (2006). Challenging deficit thinking. *Education Leadership, 64*(1), 42–45. Retreived from http://www.ascd.org/publications/educational-leadership/sept06/vol64/num01/Challenging-Deficit-Thinking.aspx

Weissberg, R. P., Durlak, J. A., Domitrovich, C. E., & Gullotta, T. P. (2015). Social and emotional learning: Past, present, and future. In J. A. Durlak, C. E. Domitrovich, R. P. Weissberg, & T. P. Gullotta (Eds.), *Handbook of social and emotional learning: Research and practice* (pp. 3–19). New York: Guilford.

Deborah Donahue-Keegan

Yuan, H., & Silberstein, S. D. (2016), Vagus nerve and vagus nerve stimulation, a comprehensive review: Part I. *Headache, 56,* 71–78. doi: 10.1111/head.12647. Retrieved from https://www.ncbi.nlm.nih.gov/pubmed/26364692

Chapter Two

Embracing a Contemplative Life

Art and Teaching as a Journey of Transformation

Jane E. Dalton, University of North Carolina at Charlotte, Charlotte, North Carolina

Contemplative life and *teaching* are not words generally joined together, especially in academia's oftentimes frenzied and task-oriented obligations. In the current contemporary educational landscape, logic and reason dominate the field, often leading to the devaluing of emotions and sensory awareness as irrelevant. Yet education is a multidimensional venture, one that draws on the full range of human capacities. Engaging in practices that move us toward our own transformation and realization of the totality of our lived experience are at the heart of teaching.

Contemplative inquiry honors the quest for a deeper awareness of the way in which educators interact with content and students, recognizing that knowledge comes through intellect but also has an embodied, somatic dimension (Kerka, 2002). Furthermore, including the arts into one's contemplative practices facilitates transformation, as the arts are deeply embedded with senses and mind-body action and reaction, a knowing and feeling that includes more of the expansive range of human experience.

Beittel (1985) envisioned a change in education and described a need for "meditative thinking, a time to protect solitude, community, ourselves as complete body-mind-spirits, and the living earth and universe" (p. 55). Recognizing the need for "meditative thinking" allows space for receptivity and a level of discernment. Receptivity in both contemplative and artistic practices is about opening to what arises, receiving and discerning what is received, and then letting it transform and deepen one's understanding, ultimately taking these insights back out into the world of action.

Viewing learning from this perspective is a transformative process, one in which people come to deeper understandings of the world in ways that help them to live with greater awareness and connection. Jungian theorists Boyd and Myers (1988) explain that transformative learning "moves the person to psychic integration and active realization of their true being. In such transformation the individual reveals critical insights, develops fundamental understandings and acts with integrity" (p. 262).

This theory acknowledges that a learner moves between the cognitive and the intuitive, the rational and the imaginative, the subjective and the objective (Grabove, 1997), offering insights and transformations shaped not only by the rational mind but also by symbols, myths, and archetypes that emerge from the collective unconscious (Boyd & Myers, 1998).

Embracing a contemplative life coupled with artistic practices blends scholarship and teaching, offering an ongoing cycle of renewal and transformation through symbolic meaning and insights. Dustin and Ziegler (2005) explain that for many artists "the 'making' of art is fundamentally an exercise in meditative seeing and doing and for such artists the practice of art was inseparable from the practice of being alive" (p. ix). This chapter aims to make a case for contemplative arts as a transformational tool to create greater awareness of the complexity and depth of the lived experience.

JOURNEYING

The notion of a journey and the universality of a quest or search is basic and commonplace to humanity; it represents the never-ending seeking for transformation from the old into the new. A Celtic term, *peregrinatio,* is a concept that embraces the notion of pilgrimage or journey. The definition, however, is not traditional in the sense of taking a journey to a holy place and then returning home with a sense of accomplishment. *Peregrinatio* is undertaken because of an "inner prompting on those who set out, a passionate conviction that they must undertake what was essentially an inner journey. . . . [I]t is the ideal of the interior, inward journey. . . . [T]he impulse is love" (De Waal, 1997, p. 2).

Palmer (1999) explains the journey of authentic selfhood as stemming from one's deepest calling, setting the individual on a path to find authentic service in the world. He expounds, stating, "Before I can tell my life what I want to do with it, I must listen to my life telling me who I am" (p. 8). The teaching life can be described as a journey, an inner prompting, that compels one into service to enrich the lives of students.

I felt the call to be of service and to teach at an early age. Over time, this journey has expanded, shifted, and altered, but through each turn I was drawn deeper into my interiority, strengthening identity and giving back to the world through service. The arts have been a central tool in my *peregrinatio*, both as a personal practice but also as a studio art teacher, and ultimately as a preservice art educator preparing new teachers to use the arts as tools for transformation in K–12 classrooms.

In both my personal life and my classroom, the arts and contemplative practice intersect. As De Waal (1997) explained, the impulse that compels and motivates me to share my passion for art and teaching is love; without it, the journey is devoid of heart. Perhaps this is what is meant by the passionate conviction to set out in the world on a journey as *hospites mundi*, "guests of the world," which involves spiraling inward to our true selves.

ART AS CONTEMPLATIVE PRACTICE

In early times, people knew well that dance, song, art, and storytelling were all part of the same process: that of the desire to create, to make meaning, and to express themselves through imagery, song, and movement, merging their inner landscape with the external world. Perhaps the arts were what the German theologian Dorothee Sölle was speaking about when she stated the need for "a language that takes our emotions seriously and gives them real weight in our lives and encourages us to think and be and act differently" (cited in O'Reilley, 1998, p. xi).

Art making is deeply emotional and can offer a way of knowing that emerges when we move our way of thinking from rational thinking and embrace full-bodied knowing. Hart (2000) defines these experiences as an emotional-cognitive process. To engage in full-bodied knowing through art, it is important to let go of the rational thought and the technicality, skill, or product needed for art making and instead focus on process of creation as purely an expressive act.

An expressive arts framework, originally developed within the psycho-therapeutic field, engages all the arts for healing and discovery with a focus on process more than product (Knill, Levine, & Levine, 2005). The framework offers an integrative approach that draws upon one's intuitive abilities as well as logical and linear thought processes, with the aim of facilitating inner awareness, self-expression, and higher states of consciousness.

Engaging in expressive arts practices with contemplative inquiry provides a bridge between my work as artist, researcher, and teacher educator. These practices (meditation, visual arts, music, and poetry) restore divisions between cognitive and affective ways of knowing, blending and balancing personal and professional identity.

Through a contemplative and creative engagement with materials and concepts, I engage mindfully with the process and experience of making art, opening to self-inquiry through images, colors, and sensations. Furthermore, contemplative arts experiences offer opportunities for understanding and working with the ever-evolving self that is continually constructed and reconstructed through interactions with contexts, experiences, students, and colleagues.

Art is a change agent. It is "an essential form of expression and communication, an expansive and diverse language fundamentally connected to experiencing and engaging in the world around us" (Polster, 2010, p. 19). Over the years, I have witnessed within myself and through observing others the transformative power of the arts; when "doing art," something happens that is both inexplicable and touches upon both my inner and outer world.

Artistic expression gives voice to our authentic selves whether visually, theatrically, and/or verbally in stories or poetry. When people begin to engage with art processes, they understand that what they are doing is somehow important on both an intimate and a personal level. It may be what Brown (2010) describes as "letting our true selves be seen" (p. 49).

Practicing and teaching art through a contemplative and mindful lens—which I define as creating and paying regular, focused attention to the present moment, materials, and process, and letting the outcome be guided by receptivity and intuitive knowing—offers tools for the journey within. Rosch (2004) explains, "Both meditation and the arts tap into basic intuition . . . meditation and art can illuminate each other and can do so beyond particular artistic styles or practices" (p. 38).

Mindfulness is about direct experience, and in the arts this is not only relevant but essential to the interaction of ideas, materials, and maker. Approaching making with nonjudgmental awareness of the present moment aids the mind in observing thoughts from a compassionate stance without berating or shaming; it is the ability of the mind to observe without criticism. In the arts, this allows the maker to take a balanced interest in things exactly as they are in the moment through receptive engagement with inspiration and imagination. This is what the ancient Greeks called *poiesis*, which translates as "to make" (Whitehead, n.d.).

Whitehead (n.d.) explains

> *poiesis* as bringing about a transforming encounter between the artist and [their] work in the unfolding conditions of art-making itself . . . working with the raw materials of the imagination (ideas, concepts, schemata) and those of the material order (paint, clay, or stone), constitutes a means of renegotiating our sense of place.

Understanding the concept of poesis from a contemplative stance illustrates how the artist and process yields insights to create a unifying and transformative practice, thereby strengthening interiority. Each experience with making, no matter the size or materials, is in essence an inward journey, a *peregrina-*

tio undertaken because of a fervent conviction to let your life tell you who you are.

FINDING INSPIRATION FROM MONASTIC PRACTICES

The work of Hildegard of Bingen, a twelfth-century Benedictine abbess, provides a source of inspiration for art as a contemplative path. She possessed an immense creative power that was revealed in art, music, and poetry, but also in her work as an herbalist, healer, and spiritual director (Paintner, 2016). She believed in what is called *viriditas*—the central creative life force that exists within each moment and that is continuously at work.

Viriditas, a metaphor for spiritual and physical health, is a guiding theme in Hildegard's work and translates as greening, freshness, vitality, fruitfulness, life-force, or growth (Hildegard of Bingen, n.d.). She saw the lushness and fecundity of nature as a reminder of divine power and interconnectivity accessible to everyone; it was not just symbolic, but a state of being that offered growth and renewal. I contend that it is also transformation.

Additionally, the monastic path of Hildegard of Bingen relied on the need for silence, sacred rhythms, and the creative arts as practices for expressing *viriditas* and connection with the divine. Most importantly, she believed in moderation and balance. In our frenzied contemporary world, I draw inspiration from the monastic path she presents, recognizing the need for balance, moderation, and creative pursuits encapsulated in moments of silence and solitude.

In these practices, the contemplative way embedded with art nurtures my interiority while simultaneously cultivating spaciousness and time for reflection and introspection. Engaging in creative acts affords a window through which I can look both inwardly and outwardly at a slow, mindful pace that does not compete with the oftentimes frenetic pace of daily and academic life.

Thomas Merton, a Trappist monk of the Benedictine, offers a reminder of the dangers and perils of a life bombarded with busyness and excess:

> The rush and pressure of modern life are a form, perhaps the most common form, of its innate violence. To allow oneself to be carried away by a multitude of conflicting concerns, to surrender to too many demands, to commit oneself to too many projects, to want to help everyone in everything, is to succumb to violence. . . . It destroys the fruitfulness of our own work, because it kills the root of inner wisdom which makes work fruitful. (1968, p. 81)

The words and practices of Hildegard of Bingen and Merton are reminders of the need for balance that includes moderation, silence, and creative pursuits.

By balancing academic work with creative art practices and nurturing the inner life as counterbalance to day-to-day outer demands, I remain connected to a creative source that is authentic, life-affirming, and "greening"; in turn, the benefits of these practices ripple outward into the classroom as I prepare preservice teachers for their journey ahead.

LECTIO DIVINA AND ARTISTIC PRACTICE

In the busyness of academic life, finding ways to engage in art making remains a challenge, yet finding time for creative engagement with small and intimate projects affords contemplative opportunities for personal growth, renewal, and transformation. I have adapted the Benedictine practice of *Lectio Divina* to a contemporary context, where through creative expression I bring together words and imagery with the aim of using creative expression and sacred reading to inform, inspire, and transform.

Lectio Divina was designed for sacred reading of scripture. This practice involves reading or listening that opens gradually to contemplation; it is considered a path of the heart (Lichtmann, 2005; Paintner, 2011b). Through a four-step process that is slow and reflective, the mind is drawn away from the preoccupations of the moment by being fully present with the words revealed on the page. *Lectio Divina* aids the movement of awareness from the rational and analytical toward a greater wholeness by including the intuitive and emotional ways of knowing.

Saint Benedict explained this process as "listening with the ear of your heart" (Paintner, 2011a, p. 18). This, of course, is not the literal ear but the center of our being, our heart, where we make meaning through a deeper connection with our inner life and the world in which we live. Rainer Maria Rilke offers a secular description of the practice to illustrate the contemplative nature of the reading: "He does not always remain bent over his pages; he often leans back and closes his eyes over a line he has been reading again, and its meaning spreads through his blood" (quoted in Lichtmann, 2005, p. 22).

Paintner (2011a) provides an adaption of the *Lectio Divina* process that extends the traditional practice and includes a visual art response. I use this model, letting words and imagery transform my way of experiencing and responding to words. Every experience is unique, and the expressive art response revelatory, oftentimes transformative, and always deeply renewing. I approach the *Lectio Divina* process similar to how I practice meditation: with nonjudgment, openness, and receptivity. I read silently from a variety of texts—poetry books, inspirational quotes, sacred prose—with focused attention on the text, allowing the images to unfold in my imagination, and then later respond artistically. No two experiences are the same.

The process of reading slowly, savoring and allowing words to be "felt" or embodied, is counter to the pace of academia where the emphasis may require grasping new ideas and concepts, oftentimes superficially skimming literature. Balance is necessary in the hurried pace of academic life; the contemplative practice of *Lectio Divina* with an artistic response provides a mindful experience, connecting me with something beyond but also within.

We learn by practice. Whether learning to be an artist or a teacher, the principles are the same. By definition, *practice* means to do something again and again in order to become better at it; to do (something) regularly or constantly as an ordinary part of one's life (Merriam-Webster, n.d.). When I embody these practices, they become central to my daily life, seamlessly integrating the personal and the professional and the inner and the outer. In turn, these practices shape my habits of being and strengthen interiority.

There are four primary movements of *Lectio Divina*: *lectio* (attention), *meditatio* (reflection), *oratio* (receptivity), and *contemplatio* (transformation) (Lichtmann, 2005; Paintner, 2011b). The following sections offer personal examples of each of these steps using a contemporary and artistic approach.

Reading (*Lectio*)

In the initial movement of reading, the aim is to cultivate the ability to listen deeply, what Saint Benedict previously described as hearing "with the ear of our heart." This quality of attention, I contend, is mindfulness—a focused attention on word(s) that speak to the present moment, connecting my inner life with the world I inhabit. As I begin, I establish a creative, inviting space surrounded by art materials: colored pencils, paint, glue, and collage materials.

I center myself with eyes closed and a focus on my breath, slow and deep, silencing the chatter of my mind. Selecting a verse or phrase, I intuitively let myself be drawn to words that jump off the page, are illuminated, and feel significant in the moment, as if they were meant just for me. Lichtmann (2005) describes this phase of *lectio* as attention, "an abiding energy of the mind that is a just and loving gaze upon reality" (p. 12).

As words resonate and connect with my lived experience, I can hold the paradox of life, not seeing it as simply black and white but remaining open to possibilities. I have discovered through this process that wisdom is not about learning solely through the intellect, but by letting the words shape me with an open and receptive heart.

Reflection (*Meditatio*)

In the second movement, *meditatio*, words are allowed to simmer and ruminate in the embodied experience, letting them unfold and reveal insights. I read the text a second time and allow what is "felt" or embodied to spark imagination. Lichtmann (2005) describes this step as "turning over and mirroring from different angles of the subjects that we attend to" (p. 12).

This step requires silence to let the words expand in awareness, allowing images, symbols, or colors to unfold in my imagination, encouraging me to go slowly and dive deeply; I use all my senses. This is what the Quakers call hearing that "still small voice within . . . the voice of our intuitive heart, which has so long been drowned out by the noisy thinking mind" (Dass & Gorman, 1992, p. 191). Reading and repeating the word or phrase that illuminates on the page and letting this interact with my thoughts, memories, or desires invites dialogues with the deepest levels of myself, allowing insights and inspiration.

Response (*Oratio*)

In the third movement, I begin to integrate knowing with lived experience, allowing for change and transformation. Lichtmann (2005) describes *oratio* as receptivity and relatedness, "that inner openness allowing us to be moved and changed by what we attend to and reflect upon, making transformation possible" (p. 12). This approach aligns with transformative learning that moves the person toward integration and realization of their true being.

In this movement, my practice is to respond with visual images using a mixed-media approach. Images are either hand drawn or cut from magazines and collaged onto paper that is either plain or previously painted. Opening to intuition and discovering symbols, shapes, and colors of what was felt and embodied in silence and reflective reading offers a complementary way of knowing, expanding the written word through visual language. With each image, I journal to recall the experience, recollecting insights, sensations, and interpretations of meaning and purpose that connect with present-day experiences.

Rest (*Contemplatio*)

The final movement, which is Latin for "contemplation," represents the culmination of the three previous movements. In this final step I return to stillness, integrating the experience more deeply and allowing both the words and the images to touch the deepest parts, transforming me from within. In this deep silence, I can discover what needs to be heard without the bombardment of distraction. I let the words and images reveal themselves through the eyes of the heart, expanding awareness; it is in this place that I can embrace my growing wholeness.

This movement is a counterbalance to the activity of *oratio*, bringing me back to the present moment. Paintner (2011b) explains that in this movement "we are called to remember who we are without focusing on what we are to do" (p. 124). In *contemplatio*, we move more deeply inward, release the need to do or achieve an experience, and simply receive.

The four movements of *Lectio Divina* are not fixed rules of procedure but guidelines that offer a transformational tool to support and strengthen interiority by listening with the deepest level of our being. A mixed-media example and reflection follows that illustrates the use of *Lectio Divina*. Each creative illustration uses a combination of paint, collage, colored pencil, or markers on a 5"x7" white mixed-media paper.

LECTIO DIVINA: A PERSONAL PRACTICE

"To be a feather on the breath of God means to yield oneself to the divine current, to let yourself be carried by grace rather than force of personal will" (Paintner, 2016, p. 165).

I read this passage several times slowly, ruminating on the words and finding the word *grace* illuminating for me. I reflected on how busy my life can become; oftentimes an overloaded calendar exceeds my capacity to function with awareness and presence. Ignoring my body and my heart, I force personal will to complete my "to do" tasks, despite signs of fatigue or stress. I become oriented toward goals and making things happen, pushing against the very loud messages I receive to pause.

Merton (1968) describes the rush and pressure of modern-day life as a common form of innate violence; committing to the multitude of conflicting concerns and demands is to cooperate with the violence. In contrast, *grace* is defined as a "special favor or privilege: disposition to or an act or instance of kindness, courtesy, or clemency: a temporary exemption or a reprieve" (Merriam-Webster, n.d.). Grace can be a reminder to embrace emptiness and meaninglessness, opening to spaciousness and receptivity.

As I reflected on the word *grace*, I was reminded of a practice offered to my students at the beginning of each semester, whereby each student receives a "grace pass." At any time during the semester, the student can use this pass to turn in a paper late, take extra time for a presentation, or arrive late to class without a deduction; the pass can be used at any time, no questions asked (Dalton & Fairchild, 2004). I realized that the forgiveness I offer my students is the same forgiveness I also should grant to myself.

Considering my own teaching practice, I realize I often favor the organic nature of learning over legalism, giving breaks firmly but lovingly, engaging in an intuitive dance, sensing when grace might help a student and not be taken for granted. For preservice teachers who eventually will be in classrooms of their own, I have found this practice teaches empathy and compas-

Figure 2.1.   Jane Dalton, *Lectio Divina*, Mixed Media, 5" x 7"

sion. They realize their need for grace may be the very gift a future student will also need.

What would happen if I stepped away from the task list on my calendar and surrendered to grace, allowing a reprieve from busyness? What would emerge from the void that might otherwise by missed? Grace in my life is a reminder to be gentle with myself, just as I am with my students, allowing space for the unexpected and letting *viriditas* to flourish. Engaging in these small creative practices such as *Lectio Divina* affords me such grace. In the *lectio* response, the butterfly and the flower are reminders of ebb and flow, of active and still, of opening and closing and spaciousness and receptivity.

CONCLUSION

As a critical practitioner of the human experience, a teacher navigates several worlds—the inner realm of his or her personal life and the outer worlds of his or her classroom, students, and school. Creative expression draws upon the vast resources of our inner landscape and allows each of us to imagine new possibilities; without it life becomes barren. Having an arts-based contemplative practice ensures I stay in touch with the gifts of the artist: paying attention to detail, keeping connected to the ordinary moments of life, pausing, looking, sensing, and making.

These transformative experiences quiet the mind, awaken creativity, and deepen awareness by expanding the emotional depth that allows for the knowing of the self through words and symbols. These symbols and gestures provide a private language and way of speaking that nurture personal transformation, heighten sensibilities, and strengthen interiority. In turn, these insights can aid the professional life by teaching more meaningfully and compassionately, and with greater self-awareness.

As an academic, I find the following definition by Merton most fitting of the *peregrinatio* of the teacher: "The purpose of education is to show a person how to define himself authentically and spontaneously in relation to the world—not to impose a prefabricated definition of the world. Still less an arbitrary definition of the individual himself" (Merton & Cunningham, 1992, p. 358).

The *peregrinatio* undertaken because of an inner prompting is an ongoing journey that can be supported through creative expression, poetic acts, and *Lectio Divina*. In turn, this awareness and these insights are shared with preservice teachers who have begun the journey of the teaching life. The spiritual practices of *Lectio Divina*—*lectio, meditatio, oratio,* and *contemplatio,* translated into attention, reflection, receptivity, and transformation—belong to those who teach as well as to those who are being taught (Lichtmann, 2005).

ESSENTIAL IDEAS TO CONSIDER

- Contemplative art practices reduce the fragmentation of academic life, restoring divisions between cognitive and affective ways of knowing.
- Artistic practices, when engaged with mindful awareness, offer tools for personal transformation that strengthens interiority.
- Monastic practices, such as *Lectio Divina*, offer a practice that speaks directly to the lived experience in that moment, offering insight and a depth of connection.
- Teaching is a journey, *peregrinatio*, and personal practices can offer tools for deepening awareness and strengthening authenticity.

REFERENCES

Beittel, K. R. (1985). Art for a new age. *Visual Arts Research, 11*(1), 45–60.

Boyd, R. D., & Myers, G. J. (1988) Transformative education. *International Journal of Life-long Education, 7(*4), 261–284.

Brown, B. (2010). *The gifts of imperfection: Let go of who you think you're supposed to be and embrace who you are.* Centre City, MN: Hazelden.

Dalton, J., & Fairchild, L. (2004). *The compassionate classroom: Lessons that nurture empathy and wisdom.* Chicago, IL: Zephyr Press.

Dass, R., & Gorman, P. (1992) The listening mind. In Welwood, J. (Ed.), *Ordinary magic: Everyday life as spiritual path* (pp. 180–194). Boston, MA: Shambhala Publications.

De Waal, E. (1997). *The Celtic way of prayer: The recovery of the religious imagination.* New York, NY: Doubleday.

Dustin, C. A. & Ziegler, J. E. (2005). *Practicing mortality: Art, philosophy, and contemplative seeing.* New York, NY: Palgrave Macmillan.

Grabove, V. (1997). The many facets of transformative learning theory and practice. *New Directions for Adult & Continuing Education, 74,* 89–96. doi: 10..1002/ace.7410

Hart, T. (2000). From information to transformation: What the mystics and sages tell us education can be. *Encounter: Education for Meaning and Social Justice, 13*(3), 14–29.

Hildegard of Bingen. (n.d.). Retrieved from http://hildegarden.com/viriditas/

Kerka, S. (2002). Somatic/embodied learning and adult education. *Trends and Issues Alert: ERIC Clearinghouse on Adult, Career, and Vocational Education, 32.* Retrieved from http://www.calpro-online.org/eric/docs/tia00100.pdf

Knill, P., Levine, S., & Levine, E. (2005). *Principles and practice of expressive arts therapy: Toward a therapeutic aesthetics.* Philadelphia, PA: Jessica Kingsley.

Lichtmann, M. (2005). *The teacher's way: Teaching and the contemplative life.* New York, NY: Paulist Press.

Merriam-Webster Dictionary. (n.d.). grace. Retrieved from https://www.merriamwebster.com/dictionary/grace

Merriam Webster Dictionary. (n.d.). practice. Retrieved from https://www.merriamwebster.com/dictionary/practice

Merton, T. (1968). *Conjectures of a guilty bystander.* New York, NY: Doubleday Image.

Merton, T. & Cunningham, L. (1992). *Thomas Merton, spiritual master: The essential writings.* New York, NY: Paulist Press.

O'Reilley, M. R. (1998). *Radical presence: Teaching as contemplative practice.* Portsmouth, NH: Boynton/Cook Publishers.

Paintner, C. V. (2011a). *The artist's rule: Nurturing your creative soul with monastic wisdom.* Notre Dame, IN: Sorin Books.

Paintner, C. V. (2011b). *Lectio Divina—the sacred art: Transforming words and images into heart-centered prayer*. Woodstock, VT: Skylight Paths Publishing.

Paintner, C. V. (2015). *Lectio Divina—the sacred art: Transforming words and images into heart-centered prayer*. Woodstock, VT: Skylight Paths Publishing.

Palmer, P. J. (1999). *Let your life speak: Listening for the voice of vocation.* San Francisco, CA: Jossey-Bass.

Polster, L. (2010). What is art? In D. M. Donahue & J. Stuart (Eds.), *Artful teaching: Integrating the arts for understanding across the curriculum, K–8* (pp. 19–30). New York, NY: Teachers College Press.

Rosch, E. (2004). If you depict a bird, give it space to fly. In J. Baas & M. J. Jacobs (Eds.), *Buddha mind in contemporary art* (pp. 37–48). Los Angeles, CA: University of California Press.

Whitehead, D. (n.d). *Poiesis* and art-making: A way of letting-be. *Contemporary aesthetics.* Retrived from http://www.contempaesthetics.org/newvolume/pages/article.php?articleID= 216

Chapter Three

Considering the Self Who Teaches

Timothy E. Jester, University of Alaska Anchorage, Anchorage, Alaska

Contemplative education incorporates practices developed in wisdom traditions from across the world and contemporary neuroscience, psychology, and philosophy (Hart, 2009; Roeser & Peck, 2009). Examples of these practices include deep listening, self-reflection, and meditation. Models of contemplative education for higher education and P–12 schools have grown in recent years. For instance, Kessler (2000) presents "seven gateways" as a framework for teachers to connect with students' inner yearnings for "deep connection, silence, meaning and purpose, joy, creativity, transcendence, and initiation" (p. 17). Furthermore, Byrnes (2012) examines compassion, integrity, and mindful awareness as fundamental qualities of contemplative teachers.

The twin purposes of contemplative education are individual and social transformation. Although social transformation is critically important and integrally related to individual change, this chapter focuses on individual transformation. According to Byrnes (2012), contemplative education is distinguished by an "emphasis on process and outcomes of consciousness raising, critical reflection or perspective changing, developmental growth or individuation" (p. 25).

Transformative learning theory elucidates these types of changes and provides a framework for understanding and supporting transformative outcomes in education. Elias (1997) defines *transformative learning* as "the expansion of consciousness through the transformation of worldviews and the specific capacities of the self" (p. 3). Mezirow (2000) identifies a process for transformative learning that includes a disorienting dilemma, self-examination, critical assessment of assumptions, and, eventually, integration of new roles and perspectives.

Although scholars have expanded Mezirow's focus on the cognitive, rational aspects of transformative learning to include emotional and other extrarational processes (e.g., Cranton & Roy, 2003; Dirkx, 2008), a primary theme has endured: Significant personal transformation can be nurtured through educational experiences. It is here that contemplative education and transformative learning intersect. Specifically, contemplative practices can create conditions for actualizing human capacities such as openness, mindful awareness, and compassion that support transformation of perspectives and self-awareness (Byrnes, 2012).

Drawing on one of Palmer's (2007) central messages that we "teach who we are" (p. 10) and his call to address the question "Who is the self that teaches?" (p. 7), it is worthwhile to consider the role of contemplative practices in the lives of educators. This theme is examined in this chapter through an autobiographical self-study (Bullough & Pinnegar, 2001) that explores my journey as an educator engaging in the contemplative practices of sitting meditation and journaling.

CONTEMPLATIVE PRACTICES AND MINDFUL AWARENESS

Sitting Meditation: *Zazen*

Sitting meditation has been a fundamental activity in my life for the past 20 years. The discovery of meditation occurred during a transitional period in my personal life when an inherited worldview abruptly collided with a vastly different reality. I was initially drawn to the simplicity, depth, and grounding quality of the practice; these features continue to resonate.

My primary practice is *zazen*, a form of sitting meditation from the Zen Buddhist tradition that instructs the practitioner to "maintain the harmony of body, breath, and mind by sitting in a stable position with a focused mind" (Sotozen-net, 2016). Zen teacher Koun Franz (2015) offers two basic rules: total honesty and not averting one's eyes. These instructions highlight the importance of bringing to the practice a stance of openness and nonjudgment and a commitment to staying with the present moment regardless of what arises during the sitting period.

Although *zazen* is rooted in Zen Buddhism, it is available to anyone. Shunryu Sukuzi, founder of the San Francisco Zen Center, presents this perspective in a lecture recorded in *Zen Mind, Beginner's Mind* (1974): "I think some of you who practice *zazen* here may believe in other religions, but I do not mind. Our practice has nothing to do with some particular religious belief. . . . Our practice is for everyone" (p. 76).

Journaling

Journaling, as another form of contemplative practice, "can help one cultivate the ability to live in the present, to become deeply aware and apprecia-
tive of life," according to the Center for Contemplative Mind in Society
(2016). One method is to write freely about external events or one's inner
experiences. My journaling typically consists of writing at least one entry
each day that describes a recent event, interpersonal interaction, strong emotion, or dream. This is often followed with self-reflective questions such as:
What story am I telling about others or myself? What are my immediate,
unedited reactions to the event? Are there connections to other situations or
patterns in my reactions or behaviors?

This approach to journaling is similar to *zazen* in the intention to look
honestly and stay with what is occurring in the present moment. Unlike
zazen, however, it is a deliberate engagement in self-reflective questions that
can excavate internal dynamics that operate outside immediate awareness yet
play a substantial role in experiences with others and myself. For instance,
when exploring an interaction with someone that evokes a strong emotional
reaction, the self-reflective process can expose my skillful and unskillful
ways of relating as well as shed light on prior experiences, feelings, or
patterns of relating that play out in the encounter. Insights gained from this
reflective process can enhance self-awareness and a sense of wholeness.

Mindful Awareness

Mindful awareness, or mindfulness, is a key link between the contemplative
practices of sitting mediation and journaling: Both practices require and cultivate mindful awareness. *Mindfulness* is defined as "maintaining a moment-
by-moment awareness of thoughts, feelings, bodily sensations, and surround-
ing environment" (Weiss & Hickman, 2016). This approach is especially
useful when dealing with challenges such as interpersonal conflicts.

An example from my work as a teacher educator illustrates this phenomenon. A student recently informed me that she would not meet an assignment
deadline due to computer problems. Given the student's history of late submissions, my immediate reactions were doubt and frustration. However, rather than hastily demanding that she submit the assignment, I did nothing for a
couple days. During this period of waiting, I noticed that my initial reactions
gave way to an awareness of my intention to treat her respectfully and provide an opportunity for successfully completing the assignment. My eventual
response was to acknowledge her reported computer problem and offer an
extended due date for submitting the assignment. Ultimately, the student did
not reply to the offer or submit the assignment.

It is important to note that mindful awareness does not magically create a preferred outcome. It does, however, engender a direct experience with oneself and reveal the wholeness of being, including strengths and weaknesses or recognized personal qualities and shadows. In the above case, my visceral reactions were distrust and irritation, perhaps understandable given this student's pattern in not meeting deadlines. Nevertheless, by approaching the situation mindfully, I was able to notice my internal reactions without rashly striking out at the student or becoming paralyzed by critical self-judgment. Although she did not submit the assignment, from a mindfulness perspective the missing assignment was just another facet of the situation to notice rather than a definitive indicator of failure.

In summary, at the foundation of contemplative practices is the commitment to honestly and mindfully see and stay with whatever arises in the present moment. *Zazen*, in my experience, is the core practice for realizing this foundation. The contemplative approach can also be applied in journaling as a way to notice and remain with what is seen or experienced. Furthermore, my journaling practice incorporates self-reflection that can provide useful insights about situations or myself. *Zazen* and journaling have been essential practices in my exploration of the self that teaches and have contributed to conditions whereby meaningful transformative learning has transpired.

TRANSFORMATIVE LEARNING

This section begins with an overview of my sociocultural background and then highlights significant transformative learning experiences revealed in journal entries from a 10-year period. During this time, aspects of my worldview shifted in fundamental ways, specifically related to schooling and my role as an educator. I attribute these changes, in large part, to experiences in cross-cultural settings and ongoing contemplative practices. Specifically, experiences in different cultural settings often created disorienting dilemmas, while contemplative practices provided a consistent form for noticing what was occurring, staying present, and supporting transformative learning. These were pivotal experiences that influenced my perception of schooling and my sense of wholeness and purpose as an educator.

Sociocultural Background

I grew up in a rural, working-class community in the southern United States where most people worked in agriculture, nearby factories, or the timber industry. The few individuals who had college degrees typically worked as teachers in local schools. Although not wealthy when compared to the broader US context, my grandparents and parents owned farmland, a situation that put us in a position of relative economic advantage.

My family identified racially as White in a community that was about 60 percent White and 40 percent African American. Racism was prevalent in both my childhood home and in the local community. Therefore, over the years, vital parts of my personal work have been to recognize unearned race-based privilege and examine internalized biases as I strive to enact antiracist practices in my teaching and community life.

Religion was a prevailing influence. My father was an itinerant preacher who maintained a monthly circuit in different rural churches, often in the hill country just north of our home. We were part of a fundamentalist Christian group that claimed to be the exclusive keepers of truth and used the Bible to justify not only matters of doctrine but also racism, subjugation of women, and the use of corporal punishment. Formal education was perceived as a threat to my family's religious worldview, a contributing factor in my parents' message that excelling in academics was undesirable. Instead, they funneled me into the vocational track in high school, where I became an adept typist but missed the knowledge and skills in a college preparatory curriculum.

Although academic learning was discouraged, my parents expected each of their children to earn a college degree—preferably from a Christian university—as a necessary step for obtaining a stable job, ideally a teaching position in the local community. Therefore, after graduating from high school, I enrolled in a Christian university that had a reputation for rigorous scholastic standards and an ultraconservative perspective on religion, gender, race, and economics. The conservatism felt familiar, but the university's academic expectations triggered intense culture shock, given my limited educational preparation. However, I resisted the urge to drop out of college and over time realized that I actually loved learning and could excel in an academic environment. Making this discovery opened a path never before imagined.

In addition to finding an untapped capacity for learning, attending this university marked my first exposure to a contemplative approach, albeit not through the university's curriculum or faculty. Rather, it occurred coincidently one evening after having studied in the library and finding a copy of Kempis's (1963) *Of the Imitation of Christ* that was being discarded. Kempis's contemplative approach immediately resonated, initiating an enduring interest in contemplative literature and practices from various wisdom traditions and in contemporary psychology and philosophy.

The sociocultural background summarized above is a vital part of the context for understanding my engagement in contemplative practices and the transformative learning that ensued. For instance, my upbringing had instilled a racist point of view and a narrow perspective on truth. I also inadvertently discovered a contemplative tradition, which served as the foundation for my subsequent participation in *zazen* and journaling.

Teaching, as had been encouraged by my family, became my career choice, but rather than settling into the comforts of "back home" familiarity, the teaching credential was a springboard for living and working in cross-cultural settings where my racist assumptions and views of reality were challenged and ultimately transformed. Selected aspects of these transformative experiences follow.

Contemplative Journaling as a Way to Understand Teaching in Cross-Cultural Settings

The first decade of my professional life was spent teaching in elementary schools in a variety of cultural settings. These contexts included an urban neighborhood with predominantly African American residents; a rural, working-class community in the South just miles from my childhood home; an Alaska Native village; and culturally diverse neighborhoods in the Northwest and Northeast regions of the United States. These cross-cultural experiences, combined with contemplative practices, contributed to shifts in self-awareness and my views on many issues, including schooling. For instance, a normative view of schooling as an inherently positive force in society increasingly gave way to a critical perspective that recognizes how schooling often imposes limits on students through racist ideologies and practices.

My first teaching job was in an elementary school in an urban community with African American students. Although I was well prepared to teach content, strikingly absent were the knowledge, skills, and dispositions needed to work effectively with students from cultural backgrounds different from my own. The Christian university's preservice program did not address student diversity. In addition, the racism learned in my childhood was reinforced in the teacher education program, highlighted by a professor who once told me that Blacks are naturally good at jumping, running, and playing basketball but they are not intellectually inclined for academic learning.

Given this background, it is unsurprising that my first teaching position in the African American community provoked within me strong feelings of uncertainty and fear. It did not take long for tremendous challenges to surface in my interactions with students. My immediate reaction was to blame the children. For example, my journal entry after the first day in the classroom stated, "*these children* have no respect" and "*these children* are extremely difficult" (emphasis added). The reference to "these children" positioned the African American students as the deficient, problem-causing Other, conceivably an attempt to make myself feel better but also a strategy that maintains structures and practices of power (Okolie, 2003). After three days, I resigned from the teaching position.

Disappointed with the outcome yet determined to figure out what happened and do better in the future, I spent the following three years teaching in schools with students from cultural backgrounds similar to mine. Teaching in these schools flowed smoothly, with a comfortable feeling in familiar environments and ease in relating to students and their families. However, at the same time, an internal desire was tugging to enact a growing aspiration to work with students and communities outside the dominant culture.

This pull eventually led to a rural Alaska Native village where most children learned their Indigenous language at home and families practiced subsistence hunting and gathering. The first several weeks in the school were challenging and elicited concerns of repeating the conflicts and lack of connection with students I had experienced in the urban school. However, perseverance, determination to learn from the experience, and the development of relationships with community members eventually resulted in a successful teaching experience spanning five school years.

While teaching in the Alaska Native village, my perspectives about education evolved, especially related to the role of schools in Indigenous communities. For instance, during the third year, and about six years after the urban teaching experience described above, a journal entry revealed my changing perspective. An administrator at the school had called a "secret meeting" for teachers to discuss how we could raise students' standardized test scores. The following journal entry was written after the meeting:

> He is wanting us to think of ways to bring up the scores. . . . I have very little concern about the test results. If we want the scores to rise dramatically, we would have to force the Western culture on them—as if we're not already doing this—or we would have to teach to the test and cheat to raise the scores. . . . He also wants us to focus on some underlying issues which he believes are the cause of our low scores. He calls them "problems." I asked him for examples, and he said, "Such things as cleanliness, language, nutrition, parenting skills, etc." He also said we have too much [Native language] being spoken in our classrooms. He wants us to tell the teacher assistants to only speak it at the extremely needed times.

My knowledge at that time prevented a nuanced analysis of testing, cross-cultural education, or the racism embedded in the principal's statements. However, the entry reveals an emerging awareness of the negative effects of colonialism in education. Specifically, it illustrates a shift in my perspective from blaming the Other to a growing critical awareness that schools often marginalize and otherwise unjustly treat students from backgrounds outside the dominant White, Eurocentric norms.

This critical awareness continued to expand and became increasingly integrated in my view of education, as opposed to what I had been taught. During my last year teaching in elementary schools, about five years after the example from the Alaska Native village, my classroom was in an ethnically diverse neighborhood school in the Northeast. By this time, my awareness of and frustration with the way many teachers and the school system marginalize students of color had peaked, illustrated in the following journal entry describing an observation of a White teacher's demeaning treatment of an African American student:

> I saw and heard her hollering at and humiliating a Black girl in line today. She [the teacher] yelled, "Why do you have your coat on? I will ask you for the third time and would appreciate you being polite enough to answer: Why do you have your coat on?"
>
> The girl responded meekly, "I don't know."
>
> The teacher shouted back, "You don't know! It is time we start knowing why we do what we do!"
>
> [My follow-up notes:] I wonder, why do kids have to be subjected to this type of humiliation? Why are they forced to attend a school where adults want them to be like good little Christian, middle-upper class White kids? I believe that much of the so-called "discipline problems" are caused by a conflict in the authority's expectations and the reality of individuals' souls and culture. . . .
>
> To hell with her and the system's assimilation tactics! I applaud the students who are themselves and refuse to meet these imposed norms.

This teacher's behavior was clearly unacceptable and sparked my anger toward her and the larger school system. In addition, a feeling of deep compassion was generated for the student and others like her who have been subjected to harsh, demeaning treatment in schools. I also recall a daunting sense of powerlessness in my capacity to change the situation beyond small-scale efforts to promote equity and respect in my own classroom. However, these observations, thoughts, and reactions played a significant role in my decision to attend graduate school the next school year with a primary goal of deepening my understanding of schooling and diversity and working for social justice as a teacher educator.

The preceding examples from my experiences as a teacher show an evolving perspective on schooling and my purpose as an educator. In addition, the entries illustrate the salient role that journaling as a contemplative practice has played in documenting, making sense of, and learning from incidents that were often confusing or frustrating. I attribute engagement in contemplative practice that was occurring in the background of the examples as cultivating mindful awareness, compassion, and wholeness, the qualities that helped me see, stay with, and gain insights from challenging experiences.

CONCLUSION

This chapter presents an autobiographical account of my exploration of the self that teaches and the role contemplative practices have played in this process. It notes significant changes in my perspective about the purpose of schooling and my role as a teacher educator working for social justice. The cultivation of mindful awareness has enabled an open and critical examination of my sociocultural background and biases. In addition, the contemplative process has helped me realize a capacity for compassion and wholeness as an educator deeply moved by injustices that schools often perpetuate through racism and other forms of dehumanization. These insights constantly inform my work as a teacher educator.

The changes in perspective and self-awareness illustrate transformative learning as described by Mezirow (2000). For example, various cross-cultural experiences triggered disorienting dilemmas that I processed through journaling as a forum for noting and making sense of these dilemmas. Over time, new perspectives and roles emerged and were integrated, as evidenced, for instance, in a shift from a deficit orientation that blamed African American students for challenges in my teaching to a critical consciousness that recognizes the structural, systemic presence of racism in schooling.

Contemplative practices have been the grounding force in my exploration of the self that teaches. *Zazen* has cultivated the ability to see and stay with whatever arises in the present moment. I have extended this fundamental mindful approach to journaling and supplemented it with a self-reflective process to examine internal dynamics and patterns that shed light on the self that teaches. Engaging in contemplative practices has demonstrated my capacity for mindful awareness, compassion, and wholeness and deepened my intention to work for social justice and treat students, colleagues, and myself with greater care and kindness.

ESSENTIAL IDEAS TO CONSIDER

- Contemplative practices can support transformative learning by creating conditions for actualizing mindful awareness, compassion, and wholeness.
- As noted by Palmer, it is essential to explore the self that teaches—contemplative practices provide a form for doing that work.
- Journaling, when practiced as a form of mindful contemplation, can offer insights into the wholeness of one's being.
- The blending of sitting meditation and journaling provides complementary practices for engaging with the present moment.

REFERENCES

Bullough, R. V. & Pinnegar, S. (2001). Guidelines for quality in autobiographical forms of self-study research. *Educational Researcher, 30*(3), 13–21.

Byrnes, K. (2012). A portrait of contemplative teaching: Embracing wholeness. *Journal of Transformation Education, 10*(1), 22–41.

Center for Contemplative Mind in Society (2016). Retrieved from http://www.contemplativemind.org/practices/tree/journaling

Cranton, P. (2006). Understanding and promoting transformative learning: A guide for educators of adults. San Francisco, CA: Jossey-Bass.

Cranton, P., & Roy, M. (2003). When the bottom falls out of the bucket: Toward a holistic perspective on transformative learning. *Journal of Transformative Education, 1*(2), 86–98.

Dirkx, J. M. (2008). The meaning and role of emotions in adult learning. *New Directions for Adult & Continuing Education, 120,* 7–18.

Elias, D. (1997). It's time to change our minds. *Revision, 20*(2), 2–6.

Franz, K. (2015). *Meditation.* Retrieved from Zen Nova Scotia website: http://zennovascotia.com/talks

Hart, T. (2009). *From information to transformation: Education and the evolution of consciousness* (3rd ed.). New York, NY: Peter Lang.

Kempis, T. (1963). *Of the imitation of Christ: Selections.* Westwood, NJ: Fleming H. Revell Company.

Kessler, R. (2000). *The soul of education: Helping students find connection, compassion, and character at school.* Alexandria, VA: Association for Supervision and Curriculum Development.

Mezirow, J. (2000). *Learning as transformation.* San Francisco, CA: Jossey-Bass.

Okolie, A. C. (2003). Identity: Now you don't see it; now you do. *Identity: An International Journal of Theory and Research, 3*(1), 1–7.

Palmer, P. J. (2007). *The courage to teach: Exploring the inner landscape of a teacher's life.* San Francisco, CA: John Wiley & Sons.

Roeser, R. W., & Peck, S. C. (2009). An education in awareness: Self, motivation, and self-regulated learning in contemplative perspective. *Educational Psychologist, 44*(2), 119–136.

Suzuki, S. (1974). *Zen mind, beginner's mind.* New York, NY: Weatherhill.

Sotozen-net. (2016). Zazen. Retrieved from http://global.sotozen-net.or.jp/eng/practice/zazen/index.html

Weiss, L., & Hickman, S. (2016). Mindfulness. Retrieved from: http://greatergood.berkeley.edu/topic/mindfulness/definition#what_is

Chapter Four

If We Teach Who We Are, Who Are We?

Mining the Self for More Mindful Teaching

David Lee Keiser, Montclair State University, Montclair, New Jersey

> Humility is the virtue that allows us to pay attention to "the other"—be it student or subject—whose integrity and voice are so central to knowing and teaching in truth. (Palmer, 1983, p. 108)

If we teach who we are (Palmer, 1997), we have an emancipatory invitation to continuously self-reflect. To mine the self for mindful teaching includes contemplative awareness, acceptance of impermanence, and personal practice inside and outside of the classroom. Through contemplation of ourselves and our environments, we are able not only to fully comprehend the practical significance of these philosophies but also to apply them within both our personal and professional lives. For teachers and teacher educators, the ability to transform ideas into action is particularly important, and mindfulness in and out of the classroom may very well serve as the key to effective instruction.

Recently, when asked to describe my path toward a contemplative pedagogy, I cited two external maelstroms: the war on terror and the narrowing of the public school curriculum in the United States; and one internal, personal challenge: both my parents had died from cancer in 2002.

Around that same time, I attended a conference, "Making Peace in Ourselves and Our World" at Teachers College in New York, that became my introduction to the nexus of contemplative learning and university teaching. I was particularly inspired by the salience of two presenters, Jon Kabat-Zinn and Arthur Zajonc, both of whom spoke to an affective and spiritual loss, and challenge in the world and, by extension, in the field of education.

Although the conference helped me to reconcile the struggles I faced in my personal life, it was still unclear how these ideologies could be applied within my profession. At the time, the relationship between my work as a professor (i.e., preparing secondary school teachers at a secular public university) and the conference's discussions and shared practices—specifically those that addressed breath awareness and lovingkindness meditation—were somewhat ambiguous to me. Ergo, I continued to investigate the connection between contemplative theory and its classroom applications with an open heart and mind.

For each year from 2006 through 2008, I had the privilege of attending and presenting at a annual weeklong summer curriculum workshop at Smith College, sponsored by the Center for Contemplative Mind in Society. This provided me with the opportunity to exchange ideas with a self-selected pedagogical group of peers who also shared an interest in contemplative practice. Through practical experimentation, we were able to modify and contextualize contemplative techniques for the classroom, many of which were then incorporated into my personal pedagogy and classroom teaching.

As a result, I increased my wait time, both in terms of how soon to effectively incorporate practices and literally, as in slowing down my reaction and response time. I gradually incorporated additional contemplative practices into my university teaching. Two of these approaches will be discussed later in the chapter.

This chapter reflects upon my development as a contemplative teacher educator. I draw from artifacts and materials from my teaching and from my own contemplative practices; from retreats and workshops with the Association for Contemplative Mind in Higher Education (ACMHE) and the CARE for Teachers program, formerly of the Garrison Institute; and from notes written during sabbatical visits to Naropa University and the Insight Meditation Society to address the question: How has my involvement with and my incorporation of contemplative pedagogy deepened my relationship to the practice of teaching and teacher preparation?

CONCEPTUAL FRAME: PEDAGOGICAL BRICOLAGE

Bricolage is a French term used to connote the process of improvisation using available objects in human creations. A bricoleur makes use of available tools, artifacts, and ideas in the creation of bricolage. These terms, often used in art and architecture, apply to academic contexts as well. For example, a pedagogical bricoleur might make use of available physical, mental, and emotional constructions and consider all objects and ideas as possible instructional resources. Similarly, a teacher educator using this frame can encourage preservice teachers to reflect on themselves and their worlds in an effort to harvest pedagogical fruit from previously untasted yet savory sources. In order to do this, teacher educators need to be sponges for curriculum and ideas, open to absorbing widely.

For example, as a former middle and high school classroom teacher, I trawled garage and yard sales and thrift stores for used curricula, games, books, materials, and even toys for my classroom. Educational material does not exist in textbooks alone; rather, it subsists in our everyday environments and experiences. Even now, I continue to glean both teaching practices and theoretical groundings outside of academe.

In fact, many of my clearest teachings have come from sources outside of school settings: martial arts instructors, meditation teachers, and, interestingly, a swing dance instructor have all reached and perhaps changed me like few academic personnel have—a realization that required a great deal of humility to accept, especially considering my role as an educator!

As a teacher educator, it is essential to present my students with a curriculum derived from multiple and variegated sources in order to explicitly model for them the creation of a pedagogical bricolage. Moreover, it is imperative I explain its connection to what is known in education as the *sponge factor*, a philosophy that encourages educators to always be open to individual learning and personal growth through an active engagement with and awareness of the learning process in any and all circumstances. Like a sponge absorbing the water in which it is immersed, they will be able to continuously incorporate new knowledge and skills into their classroom instruction.

By contemplating the instructional approaches of various teachers—including those outside traditional school settings—and reflecting upon those experiences, preservice teachers will find themselves struck by a sense of humility defined by the understanding that knowledge can be found all around them, not just in a classroom. Moreover, they will be equipped with the capacity to be constantly building a mental file cabinet of ideas, which will eventually evolve into their own personal pedagogical toolbox consisting of an array of educational strategies and resources. This will enable them not only to build a manifold curriculum but also to engage with a diverse student body whose knowledge and interests might be different from their own.

Though the experiences with the aforementioned teachers forever contributed to my pedagogical toolbox, it is necessary to remember that those moments with them were temporary and fleeting. With that in mind, pedagogical bricolage serves as a framework for me—and thus, my students—to become cognizant of teaching moments as they present themselves within the complex, ever-changing networks of everyday life.

By teaching the process of bricolage, I am equipping my students with a viable method by which they can collect, organize, and display experiences in their lives and eventually their classrooms with intrinsic meaning. Said a different way, slowing down has helped me reflect on pedagogy and the myriad strands from which I weave it. Taking time to build can help builders understand their materials. Seeing and using the tools of my teaching life in the service of students is a symbiotic form of professional development for both teacher and learner.

IMPERMANENCE

As Heraclitus suggested, "[T]he river where you set your foot just now is gone/those waters/giving way/to this" (Haxton, 2001, p. 27). Said another way, the flow of time—like the flow of water—brings with it constant change. Just as you cannot step into the same river twice, you cannot experience the same moment twice; and just as the river is different for the flow of water, each moment is different for its unique confluence of people, mental and/or emotional states, and environmental conditions.

A conscious awareness of these nearly imperceptible changes can greatly affect the way people understand and relate to a river or, more importantly, the people and world around us. Accepting it has deepened my relationship to teacher education practice and pedagogy, in terms of both the regular turnover of students, curriculum, and policies, and the inherent inconsistencies of academic stress.

As teachers, it is important to recognize the wisdom and relevance of Heraclitus's words in the world of education. Thus, no two classrooms are the same, no two students are the same, and no two lessons are the same. What is true for one class is not necessarily so for another, and even what was true for a class one day is not necessarily so for that same class a day later. Clearly, no teacher returns to the same classroom twice.

In more general terms, the sheer rapidity and immensity of structural change, the shift in employment prospects, and the continued push for testing and its concomitant alterations in curriculum make evident the impermanent nature of schooling. The continuous transformations in school administrations and policies, teaching staff and student bodies, curriculum and high-stakes testing make difficult any assumption of permanence or replicable outcomes. Nevertheless, to fully understand the nature of Heraclitus's reality opens a world of opportunity for teachers to embrace impermanence and, subsequently, redefine their approach to classroom instruction.

If we, as educators, can accept the premise that each second, each instance, each experience provides us with a new learning opportunity, then it is only logical to assume that we are in a constant state of evolution. The same can be said for our students. Therefore, to accept impermanence in the classroom is to reconsider the role of education altogether: Knowledge is considered not in terms of its end result, a grade or a test score, but rather in terms of the learning process itself. In other words, education is the development of a mindful awareness not only of ourselves and the world, but also of our place within that world as it changes from one moment to the next.

Jack Kornfield, a Buddhist practitioner and author, elucidates the connection between the recognition of impermanence and its resulting mindfulness:

> When the Greek philosopher Heraclitus said we can never step in the same river twice, he also knew that we can never meet the same person twice, that to say the word "bread" can never do justice to its shape and texture, to the unique moment when . . . we prepare to put it in our mouth. (2000, p. 294)

Life's most valuable moments cannot be taught; they must be experienced. Since individual experience is temporary, its significance may be derived from the nexus of awareness and contemplation, which is the foundation of mindfulness. Which is to say, the resolute joy resulting from taking mindful moments can only be experienced; there is no didactic replacement for a slow walk or the smell of a freshly cut rose. The acceptance and embracing of impermanence, too, can only be experienced; it cannot be lectured.

Through the contemplation of impermanence, teachers can strive to be more mindful of teachable moments that may not necessarily be the result of a well-designed curriculum or administrative policy, but rather a natural consequence of the daily interactions between teachers, students, and the process of learning. By recognizing and identifying the momentary convergence of human and environmental factors that have led to a particular circumstance, educators can model for their students how to slow down and be mindful of lessons that present themselves, if only for an instance, in everyday experiences. Students will then have the opportunity to see themselves in a state of constant evolution, too, continually learning and growing—an empowering realization for anyone.

A vivid illustration of impermanence, such as the Tibetan Buddhist practice of creating and destroying elaborate colored sand sculptures, or mandalas, evokes beauty and dedication. The process can takes hours to months, and is erased in an instant. The final release epitomizes the essence and freedom of nonattachment. The art is not produced, per se, but rather made and released.

Teachers can also provide opportunities to slow down and appreciate the transience of each moment, the impermanence of each class period or course together. Neither student nor teacher will blow away like the sand mandala, but they do need to let go of the course or class together, and each move on. Contemplative pedagogy offers the opportunity to engage with instructional practices that have the power to teach students to handle change and appreciate impermanence not only in the classroom but outside as well.

Sitting with one's breath, for example, can reveal in short order the power and speed with which we think, process, and ruminate. Experiencing the distinctness of each breath can act as a teacher of impermanence for students, and they can apply that understanding in other ways. The enormity of information that preservice teachers must process can overwhelm them. Contemplative practices can help preservice teachers, as they do me, to tame the piles of information and the incessant noise facing educators.

PEDAGOGY AND PRACTICE

Two life practices that support my teaching are meditating and writing. While the latter appears explicitly in every course I teach, the former lies stealthily on most syllabi. As a professor in a public university not directly teaching religion or spirituality, I am careful to couch my language in secular terms. To deepen my practice, I have attended meditation retreats, both alone and with other university faculty. In both cases, retreats provided an aperture of silence through which to focus and be present, observing the flow of my thoughts in relation to my environment without the distractions of speech.

Academic retreats, such as those sponsored by the Association for Contemplative Mind in Higher Education, feature both interactive and silent programming on their agendas. For those new to meditation, this may be the first "invited silence" they have experienced. University faculty are used to talking and being heard, not necessarily being silent together. But practice at taking time to be still together can steel teachers' resolve for the inevitable roller coaster of teaching students and perhaps deepen their classroom presence in ways noticeable to the students as well as themselves.

The field note below was written after approximately 30 continuous hours of silence at a 2008 retreat with ACMHE. A facilitator prompted the participants to write about the experience immediately before ending the silence, with dyadic discussions about what we wrote. My response to the experience follows:

> During the silence I discovered that much work is done there—connections made, orthogonal realities explored. . . . I discovered my need to be connected is tied very much to talk—I don't particularly like email or even phone unless it's to convey information. . . . In silence I discovered that much of what is spoken is not missed. In silence I discover myself and renew again. In silence, in silence, in silence for another minute or so.

Rare is the opportunity to write under such nurturing circumstances, and the typical college classroom does not approximate the solace made possible by extended calm, communal silence. While extended silence is less possible, perhaps, for university professors not teaching meditation, it is possible to create spaces for students to learn in compassionate community and explore apertures of contemplative practice and pedagogy (Adarkar & Keiser, 2007; Keiser & Adarkar, 2015). Following are two teaching activities that exemplify contemplative pedagogy, and encourage mindfulness in the classroom.

Creating *Pedamantras*

Nearly every semester I teach a class about equity and diversity in schools. For one of my readings, I assign a short anthology of haiku poetry. After reading poems in English and Japanese and writing their own haikus, students do an exercise intended to help them hone their teaching credo or educational philosophy. In my own experiences with what I have come to call *pedamantras* (i.e., pedagogical mantras), I have found the following contemplative writing activity to foster a deep sense of humility, in addition to an understanding of oneself—particularly concerning personal intentions, beliefs, and values.

First, students are asked to take a moment to think about the different aspects of their field. Then they write down a paragraph describing their field; most responses begin, "Mathematics is about . . ." or "In physical education we . . .". This is the concrete or objective contribution. Next, they are asked to describe themselves in the field (i.e., "I teach English because . . ." or "I will be a strong history advocate so that . . ."). This is the subjective or critical contribution. Lastly, they are encouraged to boil down their previous two paragraphs into a three- or four-word phrase. In the same way a haiku attempts to capture the essence of its subject, students endeavor to pinpoint the essence of their pedagogical stance, which fosters opportunities for personal reflection and insight.

By successfully describing their pedagogical orientation, students are introduced to the indefatigable need for clarity and precision in teaching. Functioning in the same way as a water funnel, practices such as this one can help students narrow down, reflect upon, and, in turn, communicate their reasons for becoming a teacher, resulting in the creation of their own rudimentary teaching philosophies. The total exercise can take as little as ten minutes, but during that time of focused attention—creating both text and distillation—and collective silence, they can come to better understand themselves as teachers: how they think about their field, their role in it, and the pith of their perspective on teaching. This practice has worked with other populations as well as preservice teachers (see Keiser, 2016).

Stage Exercise

The acceptance of *what is not yet* is integral to the development of teaching perspective, presence, and poise. I learned the following exercise from the CARE for Teachers program and use it regularly with preservice teachers. In short, simply standing in front of the class can be challenging for many new teachers, and the Stage Exercise can help students to overcome any discomfort at the center of attention. By modeling the exercise first, I attempt to display humor and humility in an effort to break down some of the mental and emotional barriers that make this activity so difficult.

The following exercise can be adapted in many ways, but should adhere to this basic format: To begin, a minimal "stage" area is set, with no lecterns, chairs, or desks impeding the classmates' view of the teaching candidate. Students each walk slowly to the front of the room, pause and take a deep breath to ground themselves, stand up straight, make eye contact at least once with everyone in the room, and slowly walk off the "stage" and go back to their seats. For many undergraduate students, most of whom are relatively young and not used to being stared at, this can be uncomfortable. The Stage Exercise offers students an informal chance to transcend this fear and nervousness.

As teachers, they will need to get over the discomfort that being in front of an audience often incites. The Stage Exercise can help develop the practice of classroom presence, particularly for students who are self-conscious or easily embarrassed. In their own classroom, they will often have to deal with being open and vulnerable, perhaps even put on the spot by students, parents, and administrators, and so it is important for them to learn how to manage that kind of stress and regain composure. This exercise provides them with a safe opportunity to explore feelings of embarrassment, awkwardness, or discomfort in a safe, accepting, and nonjudgmental environment.

Using Reflective Silence to Become Aware of and Address Monkey Mind

One significant difference between most P–12 settings and most university settings has to do with time: In general, primary and secondary schools are more structured, with a greater number of shorter classes. Conversely, professors must balance grading papers and class preparation with writing and publishing, work that often competes with teaching. With this in mind, it is clear why teachers and professors might feel the pressure of their jobs: an unlimited well of work and information to attend to.

As Johnson (2003) writes, *monkey mind* describes "a mind clouded by its passions and self-doubts, deluded by its own ideas, its distorted perceptions, its belief in an enduring personal identity, and its countless presuppositions and high provisional explanations about the world and others" (p. 37). Monkey mind, or distractibility, will not dissipate easily or overnight, but by clarifying our purposes and prioritizing our responsibilities, we can reduce its disabling impact.

Teacher educators aim to prepare their preservice teachers to be focused professionals, as inured as possible to external stresses and distractions, and to be effective educators with the ability to prioritize, organize, multitask, and manage time efficiently. Once these skills are learned and mastered, teachers can then focus on the real work of creating productive and positive relationships, changing their students' lives, and inspiring the next generation. While contemplative pedagogical practices like writing and meditative silence do not increase the number of hours in a day, they may create spacious time for quiet reflection in which purposes can be evaluated, steps determined, and courses of action decided upon, all of which allow teachers to be more present.

To facilitate the gainful employment of their students, teacher educators must be ready to help them still the distracting chatter of the monkey minds, the "passions and self-doubts" that make the complicated task of teaching even more complicated. *Pedamantras* can help preservice teachers to illuminate their purposes for teaching, who they are and what kind of teacher they want to be, allowing them to focus on what is truly important in their classrooms. Similarly, the Stage Exercise offers the students a chance to investigate their own feelings and vulnerabilities, without the added pressures of communication, in front of an audience. Both activities provide preservice teachers with the basic skills and practices to cope with the various demands of 21st-century teaching. A simple act of standing—while nerve-racking for some—can distill for preservice teachers the core of teaching presence. Just as trees can provide monkeys a home base to which to safely return, a strong teaching stance can provide preservice teachers a home base from which to safely teach.

Moreover, teacher educators can effectively use these two practices in conjunction to deepen their understanding of the teaching and learning process. Reflective silence prior to, and throughout, the *pedamantra* activity can help students achieve a more critical knowledge themselves and their intentions, while written responses after the Stage Exercise can facilitate a deeper understanding of their experience in front of the class. By performing the activities alongside their students, teacher educators can effectively model the use of short reflective writing and meditative silence to illustrate the power and potential of contemplative mindfulness in the classroom and beyond.

Teacher educators are in a unique position to both model and promote lifelong learning with their preservice teachers. In my experience, we can prepare for and strengthen this unique position by attending to our inner lives. Contemplative practices, whether silent and solitary, such as breath awareness, or interactive, such as practicing classroom presence together, can demonstrate our attendance with our students.

CONCLUSION

> The power of place is to locate, to situate oneself, to find again. Much like the fisherwoman plying a pole or a fisherman witnessing the ebbing of the tide, sea mind locates oneself at the edge of possibility, the risky space fraught with potential and promise as well as humility. (Keiser, 2013, p. 68)

To teach is to enter a sea of humility, an endless expanse of possibility in which forces both overt and tacit, collude and collide, creating lasting synergies. After nearly 30 years of teaching, I still feel nervous—tight stomach, sweaty palms—most eves of new semesters. Part of this reaction stems from anxiety about doing a good job, and part of it arises from the excitement of meeting and developing new classes and students.

Though teacher candidates and I will be together in class for only 15 weeks and then most likely not again, I try to present a humble, if energetic, self in an effort to help my students develop their own teaching selves. Through an active engagement with the practices I teach, I attempt to show my students that even a seasoned veteran like myself is not immune to the uncertainties that define the teaching profession, that we are all susceptible to the anxieties brought on by the world's impermanent and ever-changing nature, and that we are all imperfect human beings. Nevertheless, I endeavor to prepare them with the necessary tools to survive and thrive as an educator in the 21st century.

Accordingly, contemplative pedagogy such as described in this chapter can help to nurture space and frameworks for the process of teaching and learning. With guidance, preservice teachers can begin to harness the world's impermanence, integrating those momentary experiences into a meaningful bricolage through momentary presence and pedagogy, and to prepare themselves to teach with an acceptance of the beautiful impermanence inherent in schooling and life.

As mentioned, the central inquiry of this chapter—on how my involvement with, and incorporation of, contemplative pedagogy has deepened my relationship to the practice of teaching and teacher preparation—remains incomplete and impermanent. Through the use of reflective writing and meditative silence, I aspire to maintain a certain amount of humility in relation to my students, my instruction, and my life. More importantly, though, I hope to show other teachers how embracing contemplative practice inside the classroom, through continual self-reflection, can both enable them to teach from the heart, while modeling lifelong learning and struggle for their own students.

ESSENTIAL IDEAS TO CONSIDER

- Remind students that everything counts—their inner lives as well as their school products.
- Offer students experiences that illustrate impermanence and why this concept is useful to new teachers.
- Provide students safe spaces to express themselves verbally and in writing.
- Use contemplative silence where appropriate, and describe why and how it is being used to deepen an understanding of the classroom goings-on.

REFERENCES

Adarkar, A., & Keiser, D. L. (2007). The Buddha in the classroom: Towards a critical spiritual pedagogy. *Journal of Transformative Education, 5*(3), 246–261.

Haxton, B. (2001). *Heraclitus: Fragments.* New York, NY: Penguin.

Johnson, C. (2003). *Turning the wheel: Essays on Buddhism and writing.* New York, NY: Scribner.

Keiser, D. L. (2013). The common core of a toothache: Envisioning a pedagogy of renewal and contemplation. *Northwest Journal of Teacher Education, 11*(2), 66–79.

Keiser, D. L. (2016). Honing teaching philosophies: Creating pedamantras. *Kappa Delta Pi Record, 52*(4), 188–189.

Keiser, D. L., & Adarkar, A. (2015). Buddhas still teaching: Where is the mustard seed. *Reflective Practice, 6*(16), 1–13.

Kornfield, J. (2000). *After the ecstasy, the laundry: How the heart grows wise on the spiritual path.* New York, NY: Bantam.

Palmer, P. (1983). *To know as we are known: Education as a spiritual journey.* New York, NY: HarperCollins.

Palmer, P. (1997). The heart of a teacher: Identity and integrity in teaching. *Change: The Magazine of Higher Learning, 29*(6), 14–21.

Chapter Five

Contemplative Wait Time

Pausing to Cultivate Compassion in the Classroom

Jambay Lhamo, Paro College of Education, Royal University of Bhutan

This chapter will explore the effects of wait time, and, specifically, the extended use of the pause that wait time embodies in speaking with and listening to students. The practice of wait time and the more generalized practice of pausing during interactions in the classroom allow the teacher to connect authentically with students while reserving judgment, to be fully present in the moment, and to create a safe and healthy learning environment.

As a teacher educator for undergraduate, graduate, and postgraduate preservice teacher candidates and inservice teachers at the Royal University of Bhutan, I discuss wait time with my students and have observed its value as a contemplative practice. One student remarked about its usefulness:

> I like teachers to give me more time to think, reflect, and formulate the answer. This gives me more confidence to express my thoughts and opinions. But most of the teachers do not practice this; they expect us to answer their questions as fast as we can. (Lhamo, personal journal entry, November 5, 2012)

Those remarks touched me deeply, and I became more curious to explore wait time in my teaching.

In the spring of 2014, I analyzed my experiences employing wait time as a contemplative practice of mindful speaking, deep listening, and the outcome of an embodied presence. Daily journal entries documented personal experiences, thoughts, feelings, and observations. These contemplative practices encouraged me to practice open honesty toward myself and others while talking and listening, limiting bias or distraction. I felt empowered to look closely at my thoughts and emotions and become more aware of deeply ingrained habitual patterns of thoughts and behavior. This heightened awareness nurtured compassion, both for myself as teacher and for my students.

WAIT TIME

Mary Budd Rowe conceptualized the concept of *wait time* as an instructional variable in 1972. In the wait time method, the teacher pauses three seconds after posing a question to the class before selecting a student to respond. According to Rowe (1986), when teachers ask students questions, the teachers typically wait one second or less for a response. After the students stop speaking, they begin their reaction or proffer the next question in less than one second.

Much of the research about wait time focuses on results for students (Atwood & Wilen, 1991; Rowe, 1986; Stahl, 1990; Tobin, 1987), but I wished to investigate whether or how wait time might improve the teacher educator's behavior and attitude. I focused on how wait time could be used as a contemplative pedagogical practice to increase meaningful teaching and learning in the classroom by improving the teacher's capacity for mindful speaking and listening, as well as the capacity to be fully present in the classroom. *Being present* is defined as the capacity to be awake, relaxed, and alert in the moment (Weaver & Wilding, 2013).

It was soon clear that wait time had value far beyond the question-and-answer context. One can pause during any teaching activity, such as speaking, listening, reading to oneself or aloud, and even during conversations that happen in the classroom. The essential element of wait time is simply to stop and use a few seconds for a brief awareness practice (Brown, 2011). Wait time can be practiced anywhere, at any time.

I used this brief pause to notice my emotional state, and synchronize my body and mind with my emotional tone while speaking and listening to my students in the classroom. I discovered that this simple practice facilitated presence while teaching, which allowed me to authentically connect with students.

Being fully present with the students helps to empathize with the students' situations and see them as they are in that moment, reserving judgment. This is connecting at the heart level. For example, the transition into the first year of college is often accompanied by many challenges, such as homesicknesses and an inability to fit in. In being able to better sense their situations, I am able to teach them with an open mind, with more compassion for them and their difficulties, and therefore can be a more effective teacher.

CULTIVATING COMPASSION

Mindful Speech

Mindfulness means paying attention with full awareness to everything that arises within and around us from moment to moment. *Mindful speech* is paying attention to the sounds of our voice and listening to the words we speak or read. This contemplative practice requires one to speak with an open heart, with kindness. Mindful speech is always purposeful and calm. It can bring joy and happiness in oneself as well as in others by strengthening relationships and healing conflicts (Hanh, 2009).

Pausing is an essential component of mindful speech. By using three to five seconds to observe one's thoughts, emotions, and felt senses, an educator can observe tone of voice and words with clarity. Pausing encourages thinking before speaking, and seeing whether one's speech creates harmony or conflict with words and tone. I have observed that pausing helps me notice, nonjudgmentally, my own thoughts, emotions, or sense experiences. It simply allows me to acknowledge my thoughts and emotions as "thinking," and let them go, so I do not get caught in the grip of my own passionate or depressed thoughts (Chodron, 2003).

Most importantly, this brief awareness practice encourages me to look deeply into my deep-seated habitual patterns of thoughts and behaviors without reacting impulsively. The first step for changing any habitual pattern is to notice it. Pausing helps me see myself in the act of judgment, in the moment. It is in that moment of just noticing that I am able to experience the subsiding of the habitual tendency to judge students. Instead of a quick judgment, often based on limited information, I am able to look at students with compassion. Compassion is the process of trusting the basic goodness of what we have and who we are, and developing a more accurate understanding of other people as well (Chodron, 2003).

Compassion reinforces contemplative pausing to observe one's negative thoughts and emotions with openness, without trying to suppress or deny them. It allows the receptive mind to hold negative emotions in awareness without being reactive and impulsive. The compassionate attitude fosters positive relationship through empathic awareness by building trust and respect. Compassion is self-nourishing as it encourages opening our hearts to others (Feldman, 2006; Glasser, 2005).

As I relax into opening my heart, I am more receptive to others' thoughts and expressions, more respectful of their views and ideas. I appreciate their unique individuality and experience fewer barriers connecting with students. Following is one example where pausing influenced my capacity to respond compassionately to students on the first day of class:

> It was the first class for the spring semester and I was introducing myself to a
> group of new students. All the students were listening attentively except two
> boys in the back row who were talking. I wished they would stop and listen to
> me but they continued. I paused and looked at them with a genuine smile on
> my face. I began to observe my inner experiences. There was heaviness in the
> chest. I was labeling them as trouble-makers and I wanted to yell at them. I just
> noticed these thoughts and sensations, and let them go gently without letting
> them affect me. Seconds later, I then looked at them with fresh eyes and asked
> in a gentle tone, "Are you done with your discussion? Can I continue my
> introduction?" Their answers were in chorus, "Yes madam, sorry madam."
> Thank god! I did not fall back to my habitual behavior of using an unpleasant
> tone to respond to their behaviors. I am glad that I was able to pause and
> observe my thoughts and feelings and not react to them impulsively. I am
> happy that those two boys behaved well throughout my teaching session. I felt
> a huge sense of accomplishment for having not given in to my old habitual
> pattern! (Lhamo, personal journal entry, February 13, 2014).

I realized that whenever I speak, pausing helps to organize my thoughts and
clarify ideas in my mind as well as allowing me to slow down and create a
sense of relaxation. Choosing appropriate words carefully whenever I have a
conversation with my students is one way of practicing mindful speech. I
have noticed that pausing before each sentence gives me time to choose the
content and structure of what I am about to say.

The slight pause I insert after each sentence gives me the space to consider the next thought and this helps me to be purposeful and calm. Pausing also
helps me control my annoyed tone and allows me to speak with compassion
and kindness. Hanh (2009) rightly claims that speaking with kindness helps
to restore harmony, love, and happiness.

It is very interesting to see how pausing in the midst of speaking allows
me to listen to myself and reflect on what I say. Dass and Gorman (cited in
Welwood, 1992) discuss with great insight the importance of listening to
oneself:

> As we learn to listen with a quiet mind, there is so much we hear. Inside
> ourselves we can begin to hear that "still small voice within," as the Quakers
> call it, the voice of our intuitive heart, which has so long been drowned out by
> the noisy thinking mind. We hear our skills and needs, our subtle intentional-
> ities, our limits, our innate generosity. (p. 191)

Pausing helps me become more mindful while speaking, for example, using
an appropriate intensity, pitch, and pattern of intonation (Tobin, 2016), and
monitoring personal emotions as they emerge (Davidson & Begley, cited in
Tobin, 2016). An excerpt from my journal illustrates how mindful speaking
helps to monitor action and emotions:

Today I shared a short personal story with my students before starting the actual lesson. I paused often throughout my narration and that helped me notice the tone of my voice and my body language. I noticed my natural hand gestures, which were very spontaneous. Normally I do not notice them at all. I knew I was using too many hand movements, which could be very distracting for students. Pausing made me aware that I was making too many movements while speaking. I remained conscious, not letting myself move a lot while talking because I noticed that the movements interfered with my ability to pay attention to my speech. Most interestingly, I was able to observe my energy level at various parts of my story. The happy tone of voice was accompanied by lightness in the chest, and the sad tone brought heaviness and a kind of constriction around the chest. (Lhamo, personal journal entry, February 15, 2014)

In Bhutan, English is the second language; however, it is the language of instruction in all the schools. Being my second language, it automatically slows me down when I speak. I have noticed that whenever I am stuck for words when speaking English, pausing allows me to search for appropriate words and I am able to maintain the flow of my speech. It gives me time to think of what I am going to say next.

English is also a second language for my students, so they need a longer time to comprehend when I speak. When I slow down my speed of speaking, students are better able to understand and absorb what I am saying. I also become more aware of students' verbal responses as well as their nonverbal responses. Speaking with awareness helps me model appropriate attitudes and behaviors that have positive impact on students' learning.

Deep Listening

Deep listening is a way of hearing in which we are fully present with what is happening in the moment without trying to control or judge it. According to Hanh (2011), "In everyday life, deep listening, attentive listening is a meditation. If you know the practice of mindful breathing, if you wish to maintain calm and living compassion within you, then deep listening will be possible" (p. 11). Deep listening nurtures compassion, openness, and nonjudgmental acceptance through listening to oneself first and then to others, as Palmer (2007), describes:

What does it mean to listen to a voice before it is spoken? It means making space for the other, being aware of the other, paying attention to the other, honoring the other. It means not rushing to fill our students' silence with fearful speech of our own and not trying to coerce them into saying the things that we want to hear. It means entering empathetically into the student's world so that he or she perceives you as someone who has the promise of being able to hear another person's truth. (p. 47)

Of course, there are times when I have conflicts with my students. We often have contrasting opinions on certain subjects. Pausing to notice my thoughts and emotional state, and using the time to synchronize with my emotional tone, positively affects my ability to listen to my students. Deep listening helps to maintain balance in the heat of conflict (Hanh, 2009) by fostering respectful conversations. It brings about healing by nurturing compassion for oneself and others (Tobin, 2016). This heart-based practice shifts us from reactivity and defensiveness to compassion, which enables us to look at every individual student with judgment suspended.

An excerpt from my journal entries exemplifies how deep listening nurtures genuine confidence instead of arrogance (Chapman, 2012) by seeing values in students:

> Students were assigned reading homework. They were supposed to read and come to the class to have a discussion. I was very sure that they would have done the reading, and I was waiting in the class with excitement to start the session.
>
> To my disappointment, most of them had not done their homework, and I was not able to conduct my planned lesson. As one boy tried to explain why he was not able to do his homework, I noticed that I was not ready to listen to his explanations. I paused to observe my thoughts and emotions by taking a long breath. I noticed that I wanted to respond to him impulsively without even taking a moment to think. I saw my mind rushing to put my agenda forward. I felt an urgency to intervene before he completed his sentence.
>
> I let go all those thoughts and emotions, and I listened to him with a receptive frame of mind. That helped me look at him as he was, and I found myself being compassionate towards him and not reacting impulsively. (Lhamo, personal journal entry, November 11, 2013)

The ability to listen deeply is a skill that can be nurtured through constant practice. It is not an easy task, as Palmer (2007) shares:

> Attentive listening is never an easy task—it consumes psychic energy at a rate that tires and surprises me. But it is made easier when I am holding back my own authoritative impulses. When I suspend, for just a while, my inner chatter about what I am going to say next, I open room within myself to receive the external condition. (p. 138)

Pausing to listen deeply to my thoughts and emotions encourages me to listen with an open mind and a receptive heart to students' thoughts and emotions. I am more sensitive and attuned to what is happening as I hear, observe, and feel the other.

Developing an accurate understanding of my students further encourages me to listen to them without any tendency to judge. Such listening encourages uninterrupted space for the expression of the students' thoughts and emotions. Students are encouraged to speak openly and honestly. Many students express their appreciation when they are not evaluated and judged but simply understood from their own points of view.

Embodied Presence

Along with developing a capacity for compassion through speaking and listening mindfully, pausing helps me develop a capacity to be fully embodied, fully present in the classroom. Awareness of the body complements awareness of the mind. Both are essential. The concept of *embodied presence* is described as synchronizing mind and body to be fully present (Brown, Simone, & Worley, 2016).

Brown et al. (2016) refer to the teacher as an "anchor whose presence in body, voice, and mind empowers the students to become fully immersed in the learning process" (p. 210). Just as it enhances elements of mind, pausing for three to five seconds enhances physical presence by enabling the teacher to synchronize body, mind, and speech, bringing harmony and balance to hand gestures, body movements, and tone of voice.

Pausing while teaching, especially during lecture presentations, helps me become aware of my physical presence: the pitch of my voice, the speed of my gestures, facial expressions, and my movement in the classroom. This brief awareness moment allows me to notice aspects of presence and make changes that may promote students' learning. For example, I might notice that my position in the classroom prevents all students from seeing me. I can then move and create eye contact with everyone before speaking.

During the pause it is possible to slow down, be still, and pay attention to all the elements of presence, body, mind, and speech, without reacting to impulsive thoughts. It is this moment of stillness—which is a moment of composure, equanimity, tranquility, and ease (Worley, 2001)—that brings harmony and balance to body gestures. For example, I have noticed how a warm and expressive voice draws students in and encourages attention and listening. Additionally, a pause after speaking a few words enables me to notice my hand gestures and body movement, and synchronize them with my voice and tone.

Becoming aware of our habitual physical patterns requires constant mindful observation, as I noticed one day when I was less mindful than I wanted to be:

> One day as I was explaining a concept in class, I realized I was so engrossed in explanation that I hardly noticed my body movement and hand gestures. I reminded myself to slow down, to pause occasionally, so I could be more aware of my hand gestures while teaching. I used these pauses to synchronize my body and mind through awareness practice. They allowed me to attend to my hand gestures and I realized that I was overusing them. My actions spoke

louder than the words and I felt an urgency to avoid it. (Lhamo, personal journal entry, March 14, 2014)

Filming my teaching confirmed I had this habit. This helped me become more aware of my speedy gestures and more motivated to control them consciously while speaking. By slowing down and synchronizing my mind and body, I was able to deliver the content so that the students could learn efficiently without so much distraction.

Pausing also made me aware that I move around a lot while speaking, which may make it difficult for students to process what I am saying. Now I mostly stand still while speaking and move in silence. Moving in silence allows me to be more aware of my sensory experiences. I look closely at thoughts and emotions that arise at that moment. In this way, I am able to practice presence in the classroom by synchronizing my mind and action to nurture mindful teaching.

Slowing down and reducing my mental and physical speed allow me to be aware of what I am doing, more in control of my own actions, and more aware of what is happening in my classroom. That, in turn, enables me to come up with better solutions to problems I see, by connecting to my inner resources and being more responsive to students' needs (Brown, cited in Brown et al., 2016). As a result, I am able to better understand and manage the dynamics of classroom teaching and learning.

CONCLUSION

The contemplative pedagogical practice of pausing transformed my teaching style, changing my interactions with my students and my classroom management. Pausing deepened my self-awareness, facilitated embodied presence while teaching, and nurtured authentic connection with students.

The practice of pausing nurtures compassion in the classroom, in both the teacher and the students. If teachers are to be compassionate in their teaching, teacher educators must model this professional conduct in their education courses. In this way, preservice and inservice teachers experience firsthand how compassion supports the development of a positive and caring learning environment for students and classrooms.

Increased awareness of one's own teaching behavior allows teacher educators to consciously demonstrate desired professional conduct and articulate why certain ways of being may be more conducive to learning than others. I found immense benefit from the practice of pausing, and I encourage teacher educators to actively experiment with this contemplative approach.

ESSENTIAL IDEAS TO CONSIDER

- A brief pause of even just a few seconds provides the space to notice states of mind and physical presence, and choose more carefully how to continue.
- Speaking mindfully, listening deeply, and being fully present in the classroom nurture compassion for self and others.
- Compassion for oneself and for students changes the way we interact, promoting a more supportive teaching and learning environment.

REFERENCES

Atwood, V. A., & Wilen, W. W. (1991). Wait time and effective social studies instruction: What can research in science education tell us? *Social Education, 55*(3), 179–181.

Brown, R. (2011). The mindful teacher as the foundation of contemplative pedagogy. In J. Simmer-Brown & F. Grace (Eds.), *Meditation and the classroom: Contemplative pedagogy for religious studies* (pp. 75–83). Albany, NY: State University of New York Press.

Brown, R. (2014). Transitions: Teaching from the spaces between. In O. Gunnlaugson, E. W. Sarath, C. Scott, & H. Bai (Eds.), *Contemplative learning and inquiry across disciplines* (pp. 271–286). Albany, NY: State University of New York Press.

Brown, R. C., Simone, G., & Worley, L. (2016). Embodied presence: Contemplative teacher education. In K. A. Schonert-Reichl & R. W. Roeser (Eds.), *Handbook of mindfulness in education: Integrating theory and research into practice* (pp. 207–219). Retrieved from http://link.springer.com/book/10.1007/978-1-4939-3506-2#page-1

Chapman, S. G. (2012). *The five keys to mindful communication: Using deep listening and mindful speech to strengthen relationships, heal conflicts, and accomplish your goals.* Boston, MA: Shambhala Publications.

Chodron, P. (2003). *The wisdom of no escape.* Hammersmith, London, UK: HarperCollins.

Feldman, C. (2006). *She who hears the cries of the world.* Boston, MA: Shambhala Publications.

Glasser, A. (2005). *A call to compassion.* Berwick, ME: Nicolas-Hays.

Hanh, T. N. (2009). *Happiness.* Berkeley, CA: Parallex Press.

Hanh, T. N. (2011). *True love: A practice for awakening the heart.* Boston, MA: Shambhala Publications.

Palmer, P. J. (2007). *The courage to teach.* San Francisco, CA: Jossey-Bass.

Ricard, M. (2010). *Why meditate?* New Delhi: Hay House India.

Rowe, M. (1986). Wait time: Slowing down may be a way of speeding up! *Journal of Teacher Education, 37*(1), 43–50.

Stahl, R. J. (1990). *Using "think-time" behaviors to promote students' information processing, learning, and on-task participation: An instructional module.* Tempe, AZ: Arizona State University.

Tobin, K. (1987). The role of wait time in higher cognitive level learning. *Review of Educational Research, 57*(1), 69–95.

Tobin, K. (2016). Mindfulness as a way of life: Maintaining wellness through healthy living. In M. Powietrzynska & K. Tobin (Eds.), *Mindfulness and educating citizens for everyday life* (pp. 1–24). Rotterdam, Netherlands: Sense Publishing.

Weaver, L., & Wilding, M. (2013). *The 5 dimensions of engaged teaching.* Bloomington, IN: Solution Tree Press.

Welwood, J. (1992). *Ordinary magic.* Boston: Shambala Publications.

Worley, L. (2001). *Coming from nothing.* Boulder, CO: Turquoise Dragon Press.

Chapter Six

Sustainability through Authenticity

A Portrait of Teaching as a Contemplative Practice [1]

Matt Spurlin, University of Northern Colorado, Greeley, Colorado

Contemplative education represents a diverse array of philosophies and pedagogies derived from the wisdom traditions of the world's major religions (Repetti, 2010). It includes the cognitive emphasis of formal education balanced with the social, emotional, and existential components of the human condition that are also present in any learning experience (Zajonc, 2006). The emphasis is not just better test scores but happier, healthier, and more balanced human beings (Steel, 2015).

This operational definition provides a context for understanding the importance of authenticity in connection to the idea of sustainability within the teaching profession. In this chapter, *authenticity* refers to an alignment between who we are as human beings and what we do for a living (Stock, 2006). Sustainability—longevity—is supported by this alignment, which allows teachers, in particular, to continue thriving in a profession where only 50 percent of teachers remain in their job after the first five years (Ingersoll, 2012).

Palmer (1998) emphasizes the connection between authenticity and sustainability in teaching when he writes, "We teach who we are" (p. 15). Ironically, teachers can often experience this concept in the reverse: They lose their passion for teaching when they feel as though they are losing themselves in their work. However, it is possible teachers could find themselves in that same work by changing their perspective to a contemplative one.

This conceptual chapter provides an illustrative example of a teacher educator with more than 40 years in the profession who demonstrates that the view of teaching as a contemplative practice leads to increased authenticity and sustainability. With authenticity, the act of teaching itself can become intrinsically rewarding, allowing teachers greater probability of continuing in the profession.

A CONTEMPLATIVE CONCEPTUAL FRAMEWORK

The connection between contemplation and education is as ancient (Hart, 2004) as the activity is secular (Langer, 1989). While the term *contemplative education* is emergent in the field of modern Western education, the emergence is identified as a reemergence (Repetti, 2010). This assertion is, in part, because the concept and value of intentionally training the mind to pay attention is recognized among cultures throughout history.

Bush (2011) points out that modern contemplative education in the United States originated with the publication of William James's *Principles of Psychology*, in which he wrote: "The faculty of voluntarily bringing back a wandering attention, over and over again, is the very root of judgment, character and will . . . an education which should improve this faculty would be the education par excellence" (cited in Bush, 2011, p. 185). The benefits of such an approach would transcend the cognitive aspect of learning emphasized within current educational trends.

Psychological health, socioemotional intelligence, self-awareness, and general well-being are important for healthy, happy, and successful lives; yet not a single educational standard in the Common Core State Standards Initiative (n.d.) addresses any of these innate human capacities or how to support them in students. In today's educational climate, educators are directed to focus on student achievement, particularly on standardized tests. Initial findings in the reemergent field of contemplative education indicate the potential to increase overall student well-being *and* to improve academic performance for all students, and it benefits teachers, administrators, and parents (Burke, 2010).

Teacher educators have identified that they are "struggling with their own and their students' chronic stress, fragmented attention, time poverty, and quest for meaning" (Morgan, 2015, p. 212). Therefore, a practicing teacher educator who is aware of these prevailing challenges is well suited to articulate a contemplative approach to teaching.

This chapter focuses on the specific ways in which a contemplative teacher educator with more than 40 years in the field utilizes the perspective of *teaching as a contemplative practice* to recognize the authentic self in teaching, which demonstrably leads to sustainability (Kanuka, 2010). The key insight is that rather than merely integrating contemplative strategies into one's teaching, a more holistic approach involves the view of teaching itself as a contemplative practice.[2]

THE METHOD OF PORTRAITURE

Portraiture (Lawrence-Lightfoot & Hoffman Davis, 1997) is a qualitative method that combines the empirical observation of ethnography with the aesthetic representation of arts-based research. It highlights the participant's perspective while acknowledging the presence and perspective of the researcher in its presentation (Dixson, Chapman, & Hill 2005). This emphasis on the human element of the research process aligns with contemplative education's emphasis on the human element of the educational process (Byrnes, 2012). Consequently, this method is ideal for exploring an answer to the research question: How are authenticity and sustainability connected through a perspective of teaching as a contemplative practice?

With a focus on "goodness," portraiture intentionally emphasizes the benefits found in the data without denying their shortcomings or the limitations of the research process itself. The effect is a holistic presentation of research data that provides a beneficial learning experience for the reader. The choice of portraiture as a methodology intentionally emphasizes the benefits of the parallel goodness among qualitative research, the profession of teaching, and human beings generally. This particular portrait serves as a contemplation of teacher education so that the content and form of this chapter align to create a richer educational experience for the reader.

The participant is Mr. Norman White,[3] an elderly, heterosexual, Caucasian male. He self-identifies as a contemplative educator (authenticity) with more than 40 years in teaching, 25 of which have been in teacher education (sustainability). His pragmatic insights help preservice teachers to adopt a contemplative perspective of the teaching practice for the personal development and longevity within the profession.

Norman metaphorically describes his teaching as meditative practice: A daily engagement in self-awareness using the classroom as the cushion. Norman asserts that a contemplative orientation increases his authenticity while teaching, which continues to sustain him both professionally and personally.

This chapter includes a portrait and the corresponding analysis. The portrait is to be read holistically, as a contemplation; the subtitles of the portrait correspond with the subtitles of the subsequent analysis. The portrait itself derives from a series of four interviews conducted over the course of a month in the fall of 2015. Its arrangement is a dialogue between Norman and me in his office at his university. It presents Norman's own description of his teaching as a contemplative practice, emphasizes authenticity and its connection to sustainability within the profession, and examines the potential benefits of this perspective for teacher educators and preservice teachers.

PORTRAIT OF MR. NORMAN WHITE: GLORIOUSLY ORDINARY

Meeting Norman

Norman's office was on the second floor of an administrative building across the street from the main campus of the university. The office was small but not uncomfortable. There was a desk with only a small stack of manila file folders: no computer, no books, no paper. There was a window, but a drawn curtain blocked most of the sunlight. The bookshelf next to the window had only a stack of binders and a few stapled papers, yellowed with age. A small recycling bin and a smaller wastebasket both sat empty on the floor next to the desk. There was a small cactus in the curtained glow of the window and two handmade candles on the desk.

Hanging on the wall above the desk was a *thangka* painting, its silk border covered in an elaborate pattern of golden infinity knots. A *thangka* is a Tibetan Buddhist painting, often of a deity, used as a contemplative pedagogical device. Above my head, a framed black-and-white photo captured the image of the university's founder wearing a suit, thick-rimmed glasses, and a smirk; he was performing *ikebana*, the Japanese art of flower arrangement. Norman sat facing me with his back to his desk. His tan slacks and gray sweater were as unassuming as the walls of his office.

The sparsity of the room underscored its few decorations, or perhaps it was the opposite. Norman did not blend into the walls, but he fit in the office. The office, like the man, was a combination of Quaker and Buddhist austerities; there was an inviting warmth to both—like a space had been intentionally created for me within his own personal space. Authenticity manifested in this intentional alignment of who he was, where he was, and what he did for a living. We discussed his 40-year career as a teacher and teacher educator, and how that longevity manifested in his teacher education classes.

Authenticity

"What led you to become a teacher?" I asked. Norman's whole body remained relaxed and still, as if he hadn't heard the question.

This was a frequent response to my inquiries—the calm extended silence of authentic contemplation. He would eventually begin speaking, but his body always remained in the same relaxed position it had been in before the question was asked of him. His voice was soft and calm. Throughout the conversation, answers were forthcoming, but Norman was in no rush to provide them.

He eventually responded, "I had an eighth grade history teacher who really inspired me and who treated me in a way that respected my intelligence in a way that no other teacher had. I felt like he knew me. I remember one time when there was this kind of history contest where some of the students from the junior high were going somewhere and several of my classmates were going. He looked over at me and said, 'I'm surprised you're not going.' And I thought, 'I never thought I could be that good, to be able to do that.' It really upped my game and made me think, 'If he can make me feel this way, I want to make somebody else feel that way. This is a good thing to do with my life.'"

We sat in silence. A few moments later, I asked, "That was it?"

Norman said, "Yes. I knew I would be a teacher, and I knew I wanted to teach teachers. When I got to Collegetown and heard the Buddhist teachings about bringing contemplative practice into your daily life, I felt like there was so much potential in combining contemplative practices with teaching: not just teaching, but how you set up the whole learning environment, how you relate to everything that's going on in the classroom. I was just incredibly inspired by that.

"I've since come to pay attention to myself as a teacher on an inner level, and how I do that shifts. I'm paying attention to my different inner moods, modalities, the weather of my thinking, the stream of my emotions, and how my body feels, and to take that as context for how I'm going to be teaching at a particular time. I'm trying to be as genuine in that way as I can be. And I trust that some kind of fresh take on what I'm teaching will happen because I'm paying attention to those dimensions of myself. This is a different approach. I trust those dynamics. I trust my awareness of them, but not to the exclusion of external feedback."

He continued, "Individuality is very important in what you do in the world and how you do it. This is something I believe very strongly in terms of teacher education—knowing who I am as a teacher—so that the teacher is not divided from what they're doing. Each of us needs to find out who we are in as many different ways as possible in order to be authentic teachers. Not teaching the way we're supposed to teach, but teaching the way that's really effective and genuine for us in making a connection to students and a unique authorship of the material we teach. That's my trust in people making their own journey out of the curriculum we design."

Teaching as a Contemplative Practice

Norman resumed, "One of the reasons I didn't get that excited about school—and I think this is still a big issue, and it's one that contemplative education addresses—is that there was school and there was life, and those two things were separate. One of the most radical lessons I learned from my teacher was that this notion of work and life being separate is just such a confused attitude. We are a part of life, all of it; that's the richness and that's the sorrow. Like Parker Palmer says, 'Divided no more'(1992, p. 10).

"The idea is that if you have a teacher who is fully engaged with what they're doing and aware of how their mind is engaging with what they're doing, how their emotions are involved, how their body feels when they're engaged, then they're much more present as a teacher. They're much more available to personalize that lesson plan as it's unfolding in the class. It's a shift in focus from just presenting content to learning how to better facilitate the exchange, because it's essential that the students have a personal connection with whatever it is that we're studying.

"It can be subtle, but sometimes this attention can go quite a ways, especially when there's that engagement with the students that's happening at the same time. Because the way I teach involves the presence of the students—the participation of the students. If I'm able to be flexible in how I construct the curriculum in the moment with the students in such a way as to engage them with that material, it has a more personally meaningful outcome for them. So the great thing, for me, is to be able to empower the students—the teachers that I'm training—to do the same, and I see that happening. That is very satisfying!"

He expanded, "I think that the worldview as a contemplative teacher is so holistic and profound that it feels like you're moving from the relative world to something much more meaningful. You're not just working on the skills level, but you're working with the whole human being in a way that feels very spiritual in the most gloriously ordinary sense of the word. It is not teaching spiritual lessons but actually living the principles.

"When I was trained to be a teacher, I was trained how to do things well, how to do things effectively. To the extent that who I was as a person affected that was a problem.[4] But in my work with teachers now, I'm constantly saying that developing yourself, by developing a greater awareness of yourself and these contemplative capacities, you're going to be a better teacher even if you don't do anything different in your classroom than what you're already doing in terms of the content. A list of best practices is usually incomplete because it does not include when or how to implement those practices. So the idea of best practices is fine, but how do we apply a contemplative perspective to them?

"For example, 'wait time' is a fantastic best practice. They've proven, through research, that wait time after a question increases the quality of the responses, so it's a technique which uses time and space. But a contemplative teacher would approach it differently than one who just learned it as a technique. It's not replacing what's done in a classroom, it's relating to it in a contemplative way. A contemplative teacher realizes that, through wait time, they can move beyond the relative world—the practical dimensions of teaching—and explore new ways of connecting, new ways of exploring. Wait time becomes a method for encountering not only wisdom, but freedom!'"

Sustainability

Norman then discussed the outcomes of viewing teaching as a contemplative practice: "Contemplative education is about finding that profundity in our daily activities. You can be doing those daily activities, like teaching, without a contemplative perspective, but having one makes everything richer. From a contemplative perspective, the notion is that you learn the content, but it's not just on the relative level. In the way that it's taught—the way the material's presented—there's a possibility for a more profound experience rather than just checking it off a list of requirements."

Instead of his usual silence, Norman laughed at his own joke about rubrics, which created another kind of space in the conversation. He said, "The [preservice teachers] are working with themselves, primarily, which also transforms their instruction and curriculum. This approach to teacher education is a way to save teachers from burnout—using the inner skills they've developed in the program to decide the most effective thing they can do in a particular situation. Because I want this training to be meaningful to teachers in the present moment. I don't want them to learn a list of obstacles and antidotes that could be happening and to be able to recite them; I want them to go deeply into an issue which is alive for them now."

I asked, "Do you think that this approach could be done in a more traditional teacher education program?"

Unlike most of his responses, Norman leaned forward and replied immediately, "Absolutely. We're supposed to operate like learning machines, rather than human beings; it's a matter of bringing teaching and learning back to its roots of knowing that are essentially human and based on our natural capacities. This is sort of radical humanism; we never leave the human behind. So, it's not that we're creating something that doesn't resonate with people, in part because there's nothing religious about the way we teach it. It's secular to me in its very nature.

"Contemplative education is grounded in human experience. We work a lot with sense perceptions, with bodily experience, with simple communication—being able to listen to someone very deeply is incredibly moving. And our program attracts people who aren't teachers because they want those skills, those communications, those human relations. This notion of teaching is a very engaged, dynamic process. It's so basic to human existence.

"Passing on, sharing with—from generation to generation, peer to peer—the knowledge, skills, and capacities that we are as human beings, and developing those. There are skills around these contemplative dimensions, to these human dimensions, of being a teacher. And these human qualities need to have discipline in the best sense of the word, so that you can exercise them effectively.

"Anytime there's something that I can share with you, then there's a learning relationship, and you have a teaching role in that moment. I think that's where people lose the opportunity to find meaning in everyday life—when they don't think it matters. It's a question of awakening that interconnected, selfless dimension in human beings, which is not only uplifting personally but also for a community."

ANALYSIS: A CONTEMPLATION OF THE PORTRAIT

The view of teaching as a contemplative practice humanizes the educational process, making it feel much more authentic. This authenticity allows teachers to engage more fully in the process as a journey to discover oneself in one's work (rather than losing oneself in one's work). Discovering oneself in one's teaching makes the process both ongoing and intrinsically rewarding. This authenticity and sustainability transfers from teacher educator to preservice teacher, from human to human.

Authenticity

For Norman, teaching itself is a method for living. This insight came from his understanding of contemplative practices of a religious tradition and its practical application in the teaching profession. Norman chose teaching as a profession because he believes that one can *do* good to *be* good. He recognized the connection between who we are and what we do and took it one step further by intentionally aligning the two to create a sense of authenticity within the teaching process itself.

The emphasis of this approach lies in teachers paying attention to their inner selves. There is an innate connection between who people are and what they do for a living—that innate connection is the people themselves! However, Norman also discovered that this connection extends beyond who we are and what we do. As he stated, "It's not just teaching," but the environment itself, how the people in it relate to one another and to what is occurring within that environment. Because connections pervade the educational process, these opportunities for increasing authenticity do as well.

The transformation in the way teachers relate to themselves influences the way that teachers relate to their teaching practices, and vice versa. Because of the authenticity this relationship manifests, authority no longer resides in some external source, such as the standards or the administration, but in the teachers themselves. Contemplative teachers trust themselves and their understanding of the content, the context, and what *their* students need in the present moment. They are the experts, and they know it intimately.

Teacher authority manifests from teacher authenticity. As a result, contemplative teachers are modeling authenticity for their students. Through their practice, they are teaching students how to identify these connections and how to intentionally align who they are as people with what they are doing in the classroom as students and as future teachers.

Teaching as a Contemplative Practice

The view of teaching as a contemplative practice identifies the concepts of living and teaching as one and the same for teachers. Recognizing this connection between living and teaching creates the opportunity to continually work with that same connection throughout the educational process. Similarly, learning is the life of students. These revelations do not differ from the technical reality of the teaching experience; rather, they transform that technical perspective into a personal one.

For example, as Norman indicated, the best practice of wait time is a popular technique with teachers; however, it does not include when or how to implement that technique. How do you use those three seconds of pausing with intention? The view of teaching as a contemplative practice transforms the technical aspects of the educational process into more realistic and workable human experiences that fit a particular context.

Consequently, the best practice presented in the latest professional development is no longer a condemnation of what teachers were previously doing. Instead, the best practice is a new strategy to personalize through experimentation within the classroom before deciding whether to keep it or let it go. This change in perspective creates the space to discover the profundity that exists within one's teaching practice.

Sustainability

The characterization of contemplative teaching as a meditative practice also provides a view of teaching as an ongoing process rather than a finished product. This allows teachers to engage their teaching practice in terms of what's working and what needs additional attention instead of merely judging it as complete, inadequate, and immutable. This view encourages teachers to conceive of teaching as a continual learning process.

The process itself may become intrinsically rewarding because teachers experience the value of improving themselves, their world, and their students. Doing good makes them feel good, so they continue the work. As a result, teachers no longer feel the need to be perfect from the beginning of their careers and in every class that they teach. As Norman says, good teachers use awareness to develop themselves constantly.

When teachers are able to be more honest with themselves about what is and what is not working, they are more likely to try new pedagogies and classroom activities because there is no longer a need to make excuses for the mistakes that occur during a class. The mistakes still occur, but now teachers redefine how they perceive the mistake as an opportunity for growth and change. The difficult situations that used to cause teachers to shut down become opportunities for engagement (O'Reilley, 1998).

CONCLUSION: THE POISON IS THE ANTIDOTE

In one sense, contemplative education follows the analogy of immunization. The evolution of immunization—from the work of Jenner, Pasteur, Salk, and Sabin, among others—demonstrated that human health involves not the eradication of the disease but a fundamental change in how people relate to and interact with that disease. Similarly, teachers can thrive in the profession by changing the way that they relate to the work. The variables of the teaching and learning process, as well as the institutions in which that process occurs, remain unchanged; however, the change in the teachers' perspectives transforms their individual experiences within the process and institution.

Immunization does not involve the eradication of the existence of disease, but instead the manifestation of its symptoms within the human body. When teachers realize the pervasive humanity of the institution of education, they can embrace their own humanity within that institution. This authenticity transforms the way they relate to everything involved in the educational process. Through the view of teaching as a contemplative practice, teaching becomes learning, and learning is an intrinsically rewarding experience. The poison becomes the antidote. Moreover, the authenticity that manifests through the view of teaching as a contemplative practice leads to sustainability within the profession.

ESSENTIAL IDEAS TO CONSIDER

- Contemplative teaching not only includes contemplative practices—it *is* one!
- A contemplative perspective does not change everything, but it changes how teachers relate to everything.
- Teacher authenticity increases through understanding the humanity that pervades education.
- Teaching, like living, is an ongoing and rewarding process rather than a finished product.
- Contemplative education sustains the profession by sustaining the individual.

NOTES

1. The names of all people and places have been changed.
2. For further reading, please see Brown, 1998; Byrnes, 2012; O'Reilley, 1998; Seidel, 2006.
3. I have worked extensively with Norman in the roles of student, colleague, and researcher.
4. Norman is referring to how human fallibility interferes with mechanistic efficiency within the Cartesian paradigm, as was Anthony Burgess in *A Clockwork Orange* (1962).

REFERENCES

Brown, R. (1998, December). The teacher as contemplative observer. *Educational Leadership, 56*(4), 70–73.

Burke, C. A. (2010, April 1). Mindfulness-based approaches with children and adolescents: A preliminary review of current research in an emergent field. *Journal of Child and Family Studies, 19*(2), 133–144.

Bush, M. (2011, May 1). Mindfulness in higher education. *Contemporary Buddhism, 12*(1), 183–197.

Byrnes, K. (2012, January). A portrait of contemplative teaching: Embracing wholeness. *Journal of Transformative Education, 10*(1), 22–41.

Common Core State Standards Initiative. (n.d.). Retrieved from http://www.corestandards.org/

Dixson, A., Chapman, T., & Hill, D. (2005). Research as an aesthetic process: Extending the portraiture methodology. *Qualitative Inquiry, 11*(1), 16–26.

Hart, T. (2004). Opening the contemplative mind in the classroom. *Journal of Transformative Education, 2*(1), 28–46.

Ingersoll, R. (2012). Beginning teacher induction: What the data tell us. *Phi Delta Kappan, 93*(8), 47-51. doi:10.1177/003172171209300811

Kanuka, H. (2010). Characteristics of effective and sustainable teaching development programmes for quality teaching in higher education. *Higher Education Management and Policy, 22*(2), 1–14.

Langer, E. (1989). *Mindfulness*. Boston, MA: Da Capo Press.

Lawrence-Lightfoot, S. & Hoffman Davis, J. (1997). *The art and science of portraiture*. San Francisco, CA: Jossey-Bass.

Morgan, P. F. (2015). A brief history of the current reemergence of contemplative education. *Journal of Transformative Education, 13*(3), 197–218.

O'Reilley, M. R. (1998). *Radical presence: Teaching as contemplative practice*. Portsmouth, NH: Heinemann.

Palmer, P. J. (1992, April 1). Divided no more: A movement approach to educational reform. *Change: The Magazine of Higher Learning, 24*(2), 10–17.

Palmer, P. (1998). *The courage to teach: Exploring the inner landscape of a teacher's life*. San Francisco, CA: Jossey-Bass.

Repetti, R. (2010, September). The case for a contemplative philosophy of education. *New Directions for Community Colleges, 2010*(151), 5–15.

Seidel, J. (2006). Some thoughts on teaching as contemplative practice. *Teachers College Record, 108*(9), 1901–1914.

Steel, S. (2015). *Pursuit of wisdom and happiness in education*. New York, NY: State University of New York Press.

Stock, B. (2006). The contemplative life and the teaching of the humanities. *Teachers College Record, 108*(9), 1760–1764.

Zajonc, A. (2006). Love and knowledge: Recovering the heart of higher learning through contemplation. *Teachers College Record, 108*(9), 1742–1759.

Chapter Seven

Building Relational Competence by Training Empathy

Katinka Gøtzsche, member of the Danish Society for Promoting Life Wisdom in Children, Trainer at the Relational Competence Project, Teacher Education, VIA University College, Aarhus, Denmark

Based on surveys conducted from 2009 to 2011 with recent graduates of the teacher education program at VIA University College in Aarhus, Denmark, teachers expressed the need to develop better skills in classroom management, conflict management, teamwork, and cooperation with parents (e.g., Frederiksen & Troelsen, 2013). The new teachers viewed relationships and interaction with students as the most difficult aspect of being a teacher. They reported a need to develop skills for creating healthy relationships and better communication.

These data initiated a research and development project called the Relational Competence Project, focused on preservice teachers, in collaboration with the Danish Society for Promoting Life Wisdom in Children (known as Børns Livskundskab, or BL, in Denmark), a number of local schools, and the Department of Education at Aarhus University. Relational competence concerns the teacher's ability to engage authentically with the child or student as well as the teacher's awareness of his or her own part in creating good relationships. The preservice teachers were taught both as a group with only preservice teachers and together with teachers from the local schools and teacher educators, so that they could benefit and take advantage of the experience of these teachers.

In May 2016 the Relational Competence Project concluded four years of research and development.[1] Through this project, BL developed concrete strategies and exercises to build teachers' relational competence by training empathy. This chapter presents the conceptual and practical approach of the Relational Competence Project and then demonstrates application of this framework using a case study approach focused on a particular teacher participant.

FRAMEWORK

BL was founded in 2007 out of a concern for children's well-being and the challenges they face in contemporary society. The purpose of BL is teaching children resilience strategies to increase their well-being, presence, empathy and compassion, self-esteem, and attention. The central inquiry of the Relational Competence Project was: How can teachers, in their work with children and in preparation for teaching, increase children's well-being? An awareness was articulated that in order for children's resilience to be enhanced, relational competence and skills of the teaching professionals who work with the children would also need to be enhanced. The project emphasized reflective dialogues and training in the skills of empathy coupled with contemplative exercises. [2]

Drawing on the knowledge from developmental psychologists such as Daniel Stern (2004) and attachment theory described by Daniel Siegel (2012), this approach proceeds from the observation that a human being has social competencies from the outset. Through these, the child is met by what Stern calls *affect attunement* from his caretakers. BL also draws on knowledge from pedagogical theories pointing to the importance of a strong relationship between teacher and student across the educational sector (Hattie, 2012; Nordenbo, Søgaard Larsen, Tiftikci, Wendt, & Østergaard, 2008). BL combines knowledge from psychological and pedagogical theories with insights from contemplative traditions, specifically the tradition developed and described by the Danish meditation teacher Jes Bertelsen.

THE PENTAGON MODEL

Bertelsen, a meditation teacher and founding member of BL, developed a five-pronged model, represented graphically as a pentagon (Bertelsen, 2010, 2013; Juul, Høeg, Jensen, Bertelsen, Stubberup, & Hildebrandt, 2016). The Pentagon Model illustrated in figure 7.1 is a map of essential elements of the whole human being that can be explored and developed.

According to Bertelsen (2010, 2013; Juul, Høeg, Jensen, Bertelsen, Stubberup, & Hildebrandt, 2016), these capacities are innate, natural competencies and do not need to be learned. They need only to be brought to awareness and remembered. This map shows five different domains of the natural competencies: body, breath, heart, consciousness, and creativity.

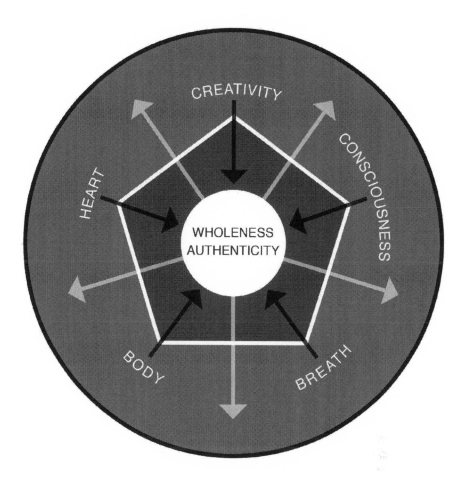

Figure 7.1. The Pentagon Model, depicting the five competencies of BL.

Every person has a body; everybody breathes from birth until death; we are able to connect with other human beings and to feel love; we have an awareness, an ability to be aware and awake; and we experience a natural creativity that enables us to react and orient ourselves in accordance with the impulses we receive from moment to moment. Every human being possesses these competencies. They are not a part of personality, because they exist before the development of personality. They are connected to the human being as such and not to the individuality of each person (Bertelsen, 2010, pp. 73–89).

Being aware of the natural competencies expands the experience of one-self in the sense that more parts of the human being are brought to awareness. It provides a possibility of anchoring one's awareness in a part of the human experience that is not affected by the patterns and limitations of individual personality.

Most of the time, our awareness is preoccupied with the area of personality. It is the individual sphere that often is controlled by the impact of one's childhood and different idiosyncrasies. Bringing awareness inward to the natural competencies provides a momentary sense of unattachment from personality, a process that creates freedom and space to view a given situation from another perspective (Juul, Høeg, Jensen, Bertelsen, Stubberup, & Hildebrandt, 2016, pp. 26–27).

BL uses the concept *to lose touch with oneself*. One loses touch with oneself when awareness is caught by the situation and the limitations of individual personality take control. In this situation, one loses contact with oneself, and one's deeper values and beliefs as a human being disappear, along with one's awareness of the natural competencies. Relational competence, as taught by BL, is to learn and become conscious of teaching situations wherein the teacher loses touch with him- or herself, and to know ways to come back to one's authentic self.

The Pentagon Model and the distinctions of body, breath, heart, consciousness, and creativity offer a reflective tool for deepening awareness and authenticity. The model can be used as a starting point for developing a teacher's relational competencies by increasing awareness in these ways:

- Body—relax the body and sense the relaxation
- Breath—focus on the breathing and deepen it
- Heart—feel the heart and show empathy and compassion
- Consciousness—stay awake and aware without having a certain goal
- Creativity—notice and respond to inner and outer impulses

The main principle in the Pentagon Model is called a *contemplative shift*. The essence of this is to move one's awareness from the outside to the inside of oneself, the inside representing all of the natural competencies, for example, to be aware of one's body, breath, and heart all at the same time. The shift occurs as one moves from acting out in the world, being an individual with a personality at its best and worst, to becoming aware of how one's body feels in the present moment, how the breath is, and awareness of one's current level of empathy for others. This training emphasizes doing the practice of the contemplative shift daily in specific settings and in everyday life.

The Pentagon Model depicted in figure 7.1 shows arrows pointing inward from the five competencies into the center, which is labeled *wholeness and authenticity*, as well as arrows pointing outward from the center. The arrows represent that by being aware, doing a *contemplative shift*, it is possible to move inward toward deeper contact with oneself and outward toward better relational contact with other people.

By engaging in contemplative exercises, one can anchor awareness in a more authentic version of oneself, where more parts of being human are brought into the field of awareness. The shift offers a possibility of being more authentic in relations with other people.

Bertelsen (2010) argues that all contemplative traditions engage these five aspects of body, breath, heart, consciousness, and creativity. They are used for:

- enhancing and developing empathy and compassion;
- enhancing self-reliance, through contact with one's inner strength and core; and
- enhancing the ability to be aware and present.

RELATIONAL COMPETENCE

Jesper Juul and Helle Jensen, founding members of BL, have been working with educational professionals to build relational competence for the last 30 years in Denmark and in Europe (Juul & Jensen, 2009; Jensen, Gøtzsche, Weppenaar, & Sælebakke, 2014). They define relational competence as:

> The professional's ability to see the individual child on its own terms and to attune her behavior accordingly without giving up leadership, as well as the ability to be authentic in her contact with the child. And the professional's ability and desire to take full responsibility for the quality of the relation. (Juul & Jensen, 2002, p. 128)[3]

From a pedagogical perspective, Juul and Jensen are pointing at different qualities that are important elements in being a good teacher. These qualities are comparable with Bertelsen's goal for contemplative training. The ability to see the individual child or to have empathy for the students, to be fully aware and present in the classroom, and to be authentic and take full responsibility for the situation—all of this takes inner strength and a solid core.

This definition of relational competence also emphasizes that it is crucial for a teacher to understand her own part in creating good relationships in the classroom. To help with this process of becoming aware, BL has created a guided dialogue exercise to facilitate connection with the dimensions of relational competence and the five natural competencies of body, breath, heart, consciousness, and creativity.

Relational Competence Guided Dialogue Exercise

In the Relational Competence Project, all participants—including preservice teachers, teachers from the local schools, and teachers from the Department of Education at Aarhus University—completed the exercise described below. In this exercise, the teacher pairs up with a reflective partner who asks questions and helps strengthen the teacher's self-awareness regarding a challenging experience.

Step 1

In the first step, the teacher describes a challenging situation with another person, for example, a child or student. It is important that the teacher reports in detail about a concrete example as a point of departure for the dialogue. It is equally important that the teacher's comments stay as close to the facts as possible. At the same time, the reflective partner is not there to offer advice, but instead to listen and to help the conversation unfold.

Step 2

In the second step, the attention/focus is turned to how the situation impacted the teacher. The following questions can be used by the reflective partner:

- What did the situation do to you?
- What were your thoughts, your feelings, and your bodily sensations in this particular situation?
- How did you connect with your natural competencies in this situation, i.e., your empathy, your awareness, your thoughts, your body, your breathing, and your creativity?
- Where were you able to maintain awareness of the natural competencies, and where did you lose this focus?

Step 3

In the third step, the attention is once again focused on the child/student in this particular situation. At this point it is appropriate to analyze what happened through the following questions:

- How can you come to an understanding of the child/person and his or her reactions?
- Looking at this situation from the child's/student's perspective, what is it that drives the challenging behavior?
- What does the child/person need in this situation? Notice if ideas arise about which needs are not being met and acknowledged.

Step 4

In the fourth step, the focus is on more skillful ways to react in the specific situation or ways to react in a future situation. The following questions are helpful:

- What will you need to practice in order to be able to respond more constructively in such a situation?
- How can you attune your behavior toward the child/student in this particular situation in a way that allows you to:

  - meet the child/person authentically?
  - be inclusive and accepting of what you see and hear?
  - get your message through?

Project participants spent 10 to 15 minutes on each step. It is possible to end the exercise after step 2 with recognition of the areas where one feels the need for practice and refinement.

This exercise addresses the principle from the Pentagon Model of turning inward with one's awareness in order to become more authentic and empathic in relationships. The dialogue partner helps the teacher to remember a specific situation and understand where his or her awareness was in the situation. When in a stressed situation, forgetting the natural competencies and becoming completely enveloped in the patterns and the limitations of personality is normal.

This process of inner exploration can help teachers to maintain leadership of the classroom and take responsibility for the quality of the different relationships and the environment in the classroom. The more aware teachers are of their own patterns, unconscious reactions, and idiosyncrasies, the more flexible and authentic their ability to engage in healthy relationships with others will be. These teachers will turn inward to enhance their ability to engage in quality relationships and develop practices to have their awareness generated from both within and outside themselves simultaneously.

On one hand, the Relational Competence Project training consists of contemplative practices, where one focuses on inner awareness of the natural competencies of body, breath, heart, consciousness, and creativity. It is necessary to practice turning awareness inward to make it natural and more automatic in situations with other people. On the other hand, the training emphasizes interactive, relational exercises, where it is possible to practice this balance of being aware simultaneously of changes on the inside of self as well as the outside.

CASE STUDY AND DISCUSSION: ANNA'S STORY

The following reflections are the result of a dialogue process such as described above with an experienced teacher from one of the local schools. The
preservice teachers observed this dialogue before they engaged in it themselves. The case below presents one example of a teacher named Anna realizing how, in her opinion, she did not live up to the definition of relational
competence. The case illuminates the implications of the definition of relational competence and the overall approach of BL. Anna was asked to describe a challenging situation with another person and stay as close to the
facts as possible. She described the situation like this:

> I teach drama. An element in the drama curriculum is encountering profession-
> al theater. That means that I arrange theatre trips for my students once or twice
> a year. I am not really good at arranging trips and I don't like it that much. But
> I do it.
>   The situation takes place a day before we are going on a theatre trip. Final
> arrangements are being made: where to meet, at what time, etc. A girl raises
> her hand and says, "I just want to tell you that I think this trip is very badly
> arranged!"
>   I reply to her in an almost friendly manner: "Why do you think that?"
>   She answers: "School ends at 3:30 pm and the play starts at 7:30 pm in
> another city. Why couldn't they come here when we finish school?"
>   I am astonished. What on earth is she thinking? I stop being friendly and
> say, "How sad! The world is not turning according to your wishes! I am afraid
> that that is how it is and you just have to learn that." I feel very good about
> myself and I can feel that the class is with me. They are all laughing. I feel on
> top of the situation. Until I look at the girl, who has tears in her eyes.

Anna's response shows a low degree of relational competence. She was
caught by the situation and by her unconscious patterns of reaction when in a
challenging situation. She made no effort to understand the student's reasons
for saying what she did. Anna did not see the girl as a full individual until she
realized that she had hurt the girl. By making fun of the girl and mocking her,
Anna relinquished her position of leadership and authority in the classroom.
She was not taking responsibility for the quality of the relationship.

When Anna realized the girl was crying, she felt ashamed of herself.
Making students cry or having the whole class laugh at a student is not
among her core values. This situation is not reflective of the way she would
like to see herself as a teacher, but she was under pressure. The girl struck a
vulnerable spot, because Anna was not very good at logistics, so she felt
exposed and inadequate at that moment. Instead of trying to understand the
girl and give her a fair answer, Anna became defensive and acted on impulse.
In the moment, she was not aware of this. She simply felt that the girl was

acting silly and needed to be taught a lesson. Anna was not in touch with her values or the feeling of empathy.

Anna had lost touch with herself. She acted reactively to defend herself, but ultimately damaged her rapport with the student. If she had responded with empathy, warm-heartedness, or a sense of curiosity, if she had had the ability to stay in touch with herself in the situation, she might have handled the situation differently with relational competence. She could have said, "You are right, it would have been nice if the play started at 3:30 pm here at school. But that was not possible, due to logistics." By doing that, she would have been authentic, because this did in fact reflect her opinion and emotional state at the time. The teacher would have *seen* the girl, and she would have shown the class that it is possible to say how you feel in the classroom without creating conflict or escalating the situation.

This example shows that in order to establish a good connection with others, a good connection with yourself is necessary. The road to the other goes through yourself. In order to strengthen relational competence, it is necessary to know how to anchor yourself in the situation to avoid losing touch with yourself. It is not enough to see the other; you also have to see yourself. This is what contemplative exercises can help accomplish.

How would it be possible for Anna to act differently should a similar situation arise? First of all, Anna needs to reflect on what was going on in the situation when she lost contact with herself. She needs to be really aware of what caused her reaction. And she needs to explore where her awareness was in the situation. How was her sense of the natural competencies of body, breath, heart, consciousness, and creativity? And how was her internal contact with these natural competencies?

When Anna did this exercise, she realized that she had a good sense of her body and her breath, but she didn't have a very good connection to her heart, to her empathy and compassion, for the girl or for herself. She thought the girl was an annoying, spoiled girl who needed to be reprimanded. In that sense, she lost contact with her natural competence of empathy and, furthermore, her ability to understand the underlying reasons for the behavior of the student.

She also lost contact with empathy for herself. Anna's feeling in the beginning was shame and inadequacy for not being one of those teachers who are good at logistics, and when the girl started to cry, she felt like a failure. A core value for Anna was to be empathic, and it was very hard for her to forgive herself for being the opposite. One way to cultivate empathy is to work contemplatively with the heart. If Anna had been able to anchor herself in empathic and compassionate feelings of the heart, she might not have lost contact with her inner values. She might have felt the same irritation with the girl, but being focused in the heart and more aware in the situation might have resulted in a different outcome.

CONCLUSION

Building relational competence is about being more empathic and compassionate with yourself and with your students. It is also about becoming more present in difficult situations, to help one remain in touch with oneself, even when feeling vulnerable and incompetent.

At VIA University College in Aarhus, BL has trained preservice teachers, teachers from local schools, and teacher educators in the approach described above. The educators have been practicing contemplative exercises with a focus on the natural competencies described in the Pentagon Model: body, breath, heart, consciousness, and creativity. Teachers have practiced anchoring themselves through awareness of the natural competencies while also keeping an outer focus—being aware of what is happening around them as well as what is going on *within* themselves.

Additionally, the teachers have been involved in conducting structured dialogues around themes of empathy and compassion so that each individual has an opportunity to explore what was challenging for him or her in building and maintaining relationships with students. Fundamentally, in order to create strong relationships, one has to have a strong awareness of oneself, an element that can be cultivated through ongoing contemplative practices, such as those described in this chapter.

ESSENTIAL IDEAS TO CONSIDER

- The teacher must take responsibility for the quality of the relationship with the students.
- To establish a strong connection with others, an authentic awareness of oneself is necessary.
- Awareness of the natural competencies of body, breath, heart, consciousness, and creativity can be used to strengthen relational competence.
- By engaging in contemplative and relational exercises such as those described in this chapter, one can anchor oneself in a more authentic version of oneself.

NOTES

1. The project is described, after the end of the second year, in Jensen, Skibsted, & Christensen (2015).

2. BL's founding members were Anders Laugesen, Helle Jensen, Jes Bertelsen, Jesper Juul, Katinka Gøtzsche, Michala Petri, Michael Stubberup, Peter Høeg, Renée Toft Simonsen, and Steen Hildebrandt. Our work has been presented in the following three video documentaries by Marianne Rasmussen.

- 2010: *Die 9. Intelligenz—die Intelligenz des Herzens. An einer dänischen Schule in die Praxis umgestetzt.* DVD Produziert in Zusammenarbeit mit den Familientherapeuten Helle Jensen und Jesper Juul, Filmkompagniet & Mathias Voelchert GmbH.
- 2011: *Mindfulness og empati i skolen: 6 øvelser i praksis.* Interview mit Jes Bertelsen. DVD. See www.filmkompagniet.dk.
- 2011: *Ro og nærvær i skolen.* DVD. See www.filmkompagniet.dk.

BL's work is also described in several books and articles.
  We have a website, www.bornslivskundskab.dk, in Danish and a website, www.trainingempathy.com, in English and German.
  3. The quote is translated from Danish (author trans.), since the book is not translated into English.

REFERENCES

Bertelsen, J. (2010). *Et essay om indre frihed.* Copenhagen, DK: Rosinante.
Bertelsen, J. (2013). *Essence of mind* (M. Bentzen, Trans.). Berkeley, CA: North Atlantic Books. (Original work published 1994)
Frederiksen, L. L., & Troelsen, S. (2013). Dimittendundersøgelse Læreruddannelsen i Århus, nr. 4: Dimittendårgang 2011. Århus VIA University College. Retrieved from https://www.ucviden.dk/portal/files/12811996/dimittend_nr_4a.pdf
Goleman, D. (2013). *Focus: The hidden driver of excellence.* New York, NY: HarperCollins.
Hattie, J. (2012). *Visible learning for teachers: Maximizing impact on learning.* New York, NY: Routledge.
Jensen, H., Gøtzsche, K., Weppenaar, C. P., & Sælebakke, A. (2014). *Hellwach und ganz bei Sich* (G. Frauenlob Trans.). Basel, CH: Beltz Verlag. (Original work published 2014)
Jensen, E., Skibsted, E. B., & Christensen, M. V. (2015). Educating teachers focusing on the development of reflective and relational competences. *Educational Research for Policy and Practice, 14*(3), pp. 201–212. http://link.springer.com/article/10.1007/s10671-015-9185-0
Juul, J., Høeg, P., Jensen, H., Bertelsen, J., Stubberup, M. & Hildebrandt, S. (2016). *Empathy: It's what holds the world together* (M. Kline, Trans.). Vienna, Austria: my Morawa by Morrawa Lesezirkel Gmbh. (Original work published 2012)
Juul, J., & Jensen, H. (2002). *Pædagogisk relationskompetence—fra lydighed til ansvarlighed.* Copenhagen, DK: Akademisk forlag.
Juul, J., & Jensen, H. (2009). *Vom Gehorsam zur Verantwortung* (Missfeldt, D. Trans.). Basel, CH: Beltz Verlag. (Original work published 2002)
Nordenbo, S. E., Søgaard Larsen, M., Tiftikci, N., Wendt, R. E., & Østergaard, S. (2008). *Lærerkompetencer og elevers læring i førskole og skole—Et systematisk review udført for Kunnskapsdepartementet, Oslo.* In: Evidensbasen. Copenhagen, DK: Dansk Clearinghouse for Uddannelsesforskning, DPU, Aarhus Universitet.
Siegel, D. J. (2012). *The developing mind* (2nd ed.). New York, NY: Guilford Press.
Stern, D. N. (2004). *The present moment in psychotherapy and everyday life.* New York, NY: W.W. Norton.

Chapter Eight

Community, Compassion, and Embodying Presence in Contemplative Teacher Education

Elizabeth Grassi, Regis University,
Denver, Colorado;
Heather M. Bair, Transpersonal Psychotherapist,
Lafayette, Colorado

This chapter describes the experience of one teacher educator who, early in her career, prepared teachers by integrating community involvement and reflection into the curriculum, and later evolved to understand the importance of compassion, embodying presence, and a contemplative approach to teacher education. The following sections describe this journey.

COMMUNITY-BASED TEACHER EDUCATION

When I became a teacher educator after 12 years of teaching in middle and high schools, I thought the best way to prepare preservice teachers would be to enhance educational theory by placing preservice teachers in the communities of their students, thus helping them understand the complexities of their future students' situations. As I looked for an institution where I could engage students in the community and involve them deeply in service, I found myself drawn to a Jesuit institution.

The mission of Jesuit education, to develop men and women in the service of others and transform learners through *experience, reflection, and action,* resonated deeply with me and my vision for teacher education. I could facilitate preservice teachers' *experience* in field placements, in the community, in school classrooms, and in homestays and cultural immersion experiences abroad. We could *reflect* together on the experiences and discuss how to take *action* in the university classroom.

I received incredible support for these endeavors at my university, but still felt something was missing. Students weren't "getting it" at the level necessary for them to be compassionate, understanding teachers for *all* students. Regardless of the readings of theories of social justice, field placements in disadvantaged schools, and deep discussions around inequities, students continued to unconsciously exhibit oppressive behavior, coming from a stance of privilege and unable to see why students did not just "pull themselves up by their bootstraps."

Rather than address this gap in student engagement with my full heart, I took the safe path, one where I felt comfortable. I deepened the community connection, hoping the community would do the work for me. I started a program in which preservice teachers studied "abroad" in the local neighborhood with families whose first language was Spanish, who lived below the poverty level, and who took in preservice teachers for a semester and taught them about their culture and language (Castro & Grassi, 2014; Grassi & Castro, 2011; Grassi & Armon, 2015a and b). Preservice teachers would no longer need to travel abroad to experience difference; they could experience various cultures and languages in their own backyard.

I believed this program would provide my students sufficient exposure to inequities to cause them to question their beliefs. The preservice teachers spent one day a week with the host families, and in most cases, both the host families and the preservice teachers expressed feelings of strong connections with their counterparts.

Teacher candidates witnessed the challenges, frustrations, and joys the immigrant families faced daily, including loss of jobs without a safety net, sick and hospitalized children, and discrimination toward family members (Grassi & Armon, 2015a and b). Preservice teachers also experienced the challenge of their own culture and language shock. Before this program, many preservice teachers did not truly understand where their own P–12 students lived and the situations these children faced at home (Grassi & Castro, 2011; Grassi & Armon, 2015a and b).

Throughout the semester-long experience, we debriefed in the classroom and engaged in deep discussion about how we, as future teachers, could better work with children who are from languages and cultures different from that of the teacher. We brainstormed strategies to better engage and involve families. We practiced instructional strategies to make the content more comprehensible to children who were just learning English and more relevant to children from diverse cultures.

Preservice teachers were enthusiastic and eager, feeling empowered to impact the future of education by the strategies they were learning and their experience with the families. Data collected on the program found trends indicating students' deeper understanding of what it meant for children and families to negotiate the US school system in a language and culture other than their own (Castro & Grassi, 2014; Grassi & Castro, 2011; Grassi & Armon, 2015a and b). I thought I was developing teachers who could connect on a deeper level.

But year after year, regardless of the strategies I tried, regardless of the reflections and deep discussions we engaged in, there were always a few students who resisted this experience: students who could never change their power paradigm, who could not see value in the program if they were not in power, providing service to families. And even more distressing was the number of preservice teachers who readily took jobs in high-need schools only to quit two or three years later. What was the missing link? Why didn't they have the tools or skills to respond to these challenges?

FROM ACTION TO NONACTION

I now realize that I wasn't engaged emotionally, and so had never provided a role model for my students to open up to the inner dimensions of their emotional selves. Never once did I stop and ask the preservice teachers to *feel* what they experienced. In class discussions, preservice teachers would touch upon their distress: Why would God let this happen to the family? How can people not see what these families go through? The whole class would nod in agreement. And then we would move on: What action steps can we take? How can we improve the situation? We brainstormed strategies, we came up with game plans, all of which should have worked in any classroom.

But we did not *feel* the sadness and hopelessness preservice teachers experienced when family members were sick or lost their jobs. We did not *feel* the love many teacher candidates developed for their host families. We did not discuss the deep fear preservice teachers had of not really being able to help once they were teachers. We just looked to action. And my identity rooted in an "action-oriented, community-based professor" propelled me forward in this direction.

I was preparing high-quality teachers who were well versed in inclusive strategies and justice education, who were willing and able to compassionately engage with students, but I was not preparing teachers to stop, feel, and engage with themselves. As a teacher educator, I was missing self-compassion and embodiment of emotions practiced by many Buddhist-inspired teachers and neuroscientists (Hanson, 2013; Jennings, 2015; Salzberg, 2014). I had not yet learned about introspection, and the power that comes from pausing, feeling, and embodying the experience.

After 10 years running the "study abroad in the neighborhood" program, I took a leave of absence to set up a contemplative teacher licensure program at a Buddhist-inspired university. I looked forward to embracing this opportunity and learning as much as possible about mindfulness and contemplative education. I started by deepening my meditation practice.

I worked with a meditation teacher at the university and attended conferences on mindfulness and the neuroscience of meditation and mindfulness practices. I watched contemplative practices in action in department meetings, faculty meetings, and with student-to-faculty interaction. I noticed a deep difference in "business as usual" at the Buddhist-inspired university: People often paused and took time and space to look internally and notice what they were feeling, thinking, or sensing.

I found this curious: There was little to no action involved. How could people possibly benefit from stopping to tune in? How does doing so change the situation? It wasn't until engaging in a conversation with a psychology professor at the Buddhist-inspired university that I began to understand the power of compassion, of feeling with another, and finally saw the missing link in the work I was doing at the Jesuit university.

COMPASSION: FROM "FEELING" (SMALL F) TO "FEELING" (CAPITAL F)

Young children often provide excellent fodder for the practice of staying in the present. For instance, I have a nephew who has dramatic, vociferous breakdowns. After one of his epic episodes, I told the psychology professor at the Buddhist-inspired university that as I dealt with this breakdown, I felt it, stayed present, and regulated my response. But I did not know what came next. He looked at me and said, "It doesn't work until you really feel it." I couldn't believe it! What did he think I was doing? I noticed my bodily sensations: my stomach clenching, my head pounding. If that is not feeling, what is?

Studying the work of teachers such as Tara Brach, Jack Kornfield, Sharon Salzberg, and Rick Hanson; maintaining a continual meditation practice; and spending another year at the Buddhist-inspired university finally helped me understand what the professor was referring to. I had to go beyond my *intellectual perception* of emotions and bodily sensations to actually *sensing* and *embodying* the feelings. I had to move beyond my thoughts around my emotions and *feel* my emotions within my body to be able to understand them and befriend them. I learned to sit with discomfort, feel it in every cell of my body, and let it be. I began to feel how emotions like sadness, grief, fear, or happiness come and go like waves in the ocean. I allowed my body to react to my experience with tears, clenching, anxiety, or whatever came up. I finally grasped the insight that I always moved to action to avoid feeling because I was so afraid of sitting in discomfort.

My nephew broke down again with me, but this time I sat with my feelings and discomfort. At first, I felt frustration, but as I continued to sit with the discomfort, examining where and how it manifested in my body, I realized it was *fear* I was feeling. This little boy was in distress and I could not find a way to help him. I was scared for him.

Getting to the root of what I was feeling suddenly changed everything. "Oh, this is fear again," I thought, "I can work with this." And when I approached my nephew while embodying my fear (rather than trying to push it away), I stopped *reacting* and making the situation worse. Rather than try to stop the yelling, I mindfully listened, and I listened deeply for as long as it took for him to feel heard. Once he felt heard, he calmed down and was at peace. I realized I could act from embodied emotion; I could both feel my fear and find a way to calm him.

Through the process of embodying emotions and sitting in discomfort, I learned something surprising: The discomfort dissipates. Emotions, even very strong emotions, last only around 90 seconds in the body—if one really feels them (Bolte Taylor, 2009). But as long as one avoids emotions, tries to make them go away, or continues telling a story about them, they persist. The patterns associated with avoidance or rumination persist, and the reactions to triggers persist. When my discomfort dissipated with my nephew, my fear around feeling emotions dissipated as well, and I was able to take action in a responsive manner.

I found that embodying one's emotions can provide powerful feedback and insight. One can actually teach from a standpoint of strong emotions. Before taking action, it is important to embody the experience, including authentically feeling the emotions, so we can create more capacity in ourselves to respond (not *react*) to situations appropriately, and to take action. Reflecting on my career as an educator, what a difference I could have experienced in the quality of my teaching as a young K–12 teacher if I had listened to my body and *responded*, rather than *reacted*, to students.

This was an epiphany for me. I realized I had spent 12 years in public schools and 14 years in academia avoiding students' and my own emotions because I was afraid. I'm not a psychologist, I'm a teacher. While we are told to care for the whole person, I didn't think that involved dealing with strong emotions. I didn't understand that truly feeling and sitting with discomfort is the only way to get through it. I was afraid of students' emotions, and I was afraid of my own emotions as a teacher.

Years ago when I was teaching middle school, a student came to me and told me he was being jumped into a gang that night. I provided strong advice against this move, but I never asked him what he was feeling. I never stopped to notice or articulate my own distress. This child had been a student of mine for three years, I knew him well, and I had great hopes for his future.

If I were to repeat this situation now, I would articulate my fear to this student with my whole heart. I would let him know that I was afraid for him and that I saw a bright future for him. And perhaps, if I had named my fear, I would have given space for the student to name his own fear. When people can name their fear, sadness, or grief, they don't have to hide anymore. They don't have to pretend that everything is okay. This student came to me for that guidance. But I didn't have the tools to open that space for him. And I needed the tools to take care of myself in the process.

EMBODYING PRESENCE IN TEACHER EDUCATION

Encouraging students to explore their first-person, inner self can be scary business in an academic setting. As Grace (2011) states, "third-person theoretical 'outsider' knowledge is often more trusted in the academy than first-person experiential 'insider' knowledge" (p. 47). Grace goes on to explain that there is deep knowledge in the first-person perspective which can inform and expand third-person views: "Theoretical (third-person) knowledge is valuable, but actualized (first-person) knowledge transmits certitude. In other words, lived truth transmits a clarifying coherence on the nonverbal level" (p. 48).

I attempted to incorporate my learning from the Buddhist-inspired university into my Jesuit institution teaching. I started by incorporating different meditation practices into my education classes to help students start to pause and feel. These practices included mindfulness of breath, sound, feeling, and lovingkindness (a practice of repeating positive phrases toward yourself and others, such as "May I be safe, be happy, be healthy," or "May you be safe, be happy, be healthy"). We started every class with one-minute practices, noticing, for example, our body, the sounds around us, our breath, and also when our mind wandered. We progressed to 15 minutes per day.

I also started class with exercises to increase emotional awareness, such as RAIN: Recognition, Acceptance, Investigation, and Nonidentification (Brach, 2012; Salzberg, 2014). Students were invited to imagine a difficult situation and then become aware of any emotions in their body: Where is the emotion located in your body? What does it feel like? Is there a story line behind it? What are you telling yourself about this situation and emotion? Can you feel this emotion without judgment? Can you just sit with this emotion?

We started incorporating these exercises when discussing textual theory on injustices in education: Do the readings evoke any emotions? Where do you feel the emotions? How do you feel them? Can you sit with them? We then progressed to using RAIN to discover feelings about teaching: Do preservice teachers have any emotions around this? Where do they feel the emotions? Is there a story line behind the emotions?

Finally, we used mindfulness exercises while reflecting on the experience of interacting with college peers in my classroom. When I observed preservice teachers practicing lessons in my classroom, we would start each coaching session with mindful noticing. How did that short lesson feel to you? Where and how do you feel those emotions? Can you sit with them? In the future, I plan to incorporate this approach when observing and coaching prospective teachers in their school-based field placements.

Once preservice teachers started to feel their emotions in the K–12 classroom—especially their emotions with difficult students—we then examined the knowledge and information our emotions gave us. We examined how we were triggered and how we could respond to the trigger in a productive manner, rather than reacting. We also took into account the child's experience and the potential suffering that encouraged the child to act out (Jennings, 2015).

I readily shared my own feelings with students so they would have a role model for moving to a deeper, inner perspective. For example, if I was nervous about teaching a new lesson, instead of falling into my typical pattern of "leaving my body and feeling nothing," I examined my feelings with RAIN. I then let students know how I felt ("I'm feeling anxious about this lesson today"), where I felt it ("I feel a knot in the pit of my stomach"), the story line behind it ("I think I'm nervous because I am trying something new and I'm afraid you won't like it"), and how I was dealing with the feelings ("I will pause at intervals to acknowledge my anxiety, but I am going ahead with the lesson").

By doing this, I not only modeled "talking about feelings in the classroom," but I continually reinforced my own journey into embodying emotions in the classroom. I encouraged personal experience (or first-person perspective) in discussions and in reflective papers about the preservice teachers' experience. I let students know that while text-based knowledge (or third-person perspective) is important, our first-person perspective also contains deep knowledge that should be explored.

When a preservice teacher brought up a particularly difficult situation (children coming to school hungry or scared), rather than moving to action immediately, we used RAIN to recognize our feelings, accept what was there, investigate how it felt, sit with the discomfort nonjudgmentally, and feel it. We stopped trying to fix it right away, waited until we understood how it felt, and explored any thoughts or stories behind the feelings.

I incorporated practices in self-compassion to address and support students' emotional awareness and capacity for emotional regulation. Students often feel uncomfortable with the oppressive thoughts or emotions they have been exposed to, taught, and often unconsciously believe about themselves, particular groups of people, or ideas. We practiced authentically examining these thoughts and beliefs, and talking to ourselves as we would talk to a good friend, sending lovingkindness to ourselves on our journey toward learning. For example, I had one student tell herself every time a negative thought emerged, "It's okay. You are learning, we are all learning. Now that you know these thoughts, now they can change."

In teacher education, we want future teachers to examine their belief systems. We try to guide them toward nonoppressive and nondiscriminatory beliefs to enable them to be effective educators. Unless students can explore their inner worlds with curiosity and compassion as they move forward to more constructive beliefs, sometimes they become stuck and their development falters.

After incorporating contemplative practices in teacher education courses, I became aware of some shifts in the preservice teachers. By expressing my own emotions and compassion, and explicitly teaching socioemotional skills, I opened a space for my students. They often stopped hiding behind unconscious thoughts or emotions. Real emotions and story lines emerged. Resistant preservice teachers found voice to express their fears and distress upon entering a classroom: What if their students laughed at them, or were not interested in the lesson? What if they failed? Preservice teachers became vulnerable with each other and discussed their failed lessons and how they felt about them.

Preservice teachers began to understand that feeling their own emotions and sitting with the discomfort made them stronger teachers and helped them to see the path to action more clearly. Preservice teachers began to translate this knowledge into practice. They realized that if they could feel, for example, their frustration or nervousness around students who refuse to pay attention or are disruptive, they can give themselves space to pause and respond to students, rather than reacting impulsively.

CONCLUSION

As I move forward in my evolving identity as a teacher educator, I hope to develop a new vision of teacher preparation, one that fully incorporates both the Jesuit call to *experience, reflection, and action,* in combination with the Buddhist-inspired *mindful noticing, acceptance, and self-compassion.* I want my students to take action, but action that is supported by the benefits of deep contemplation and reflection in the Buddhist tradition, including embodiment of the whole experience and self-compassion.

Throughout this evolution, I have been reflecting on the following questions around teacher education:

- How can teacher educators encourage preservice teachers to reflect not only on the experience *without*, but also on the experience *within*?
- How can we support preservice teachers' compassion as they wrestle with experiences and feelings both in and out of the classroom?
- How can we share tools with preservice teachers to stop, notice, hold, and embody deep emotions while moving toward action in the service of others?

When teachers take action through the study and practice of relevant instructional strategies to meet the needs of diverse learners, they become strong teachers. When teachers combine these skills with contemplative noticing, embodiment, and self-compassion, I anticipate deeply engaged, authentic teachers who are able to hold students in the present moment and stay present with themselves throughout the chaos and uncertainty of teaching.

Strong instructional strategies combined with contemplative skills do not make teaching easier. Rather, this combination provides space for a pause, a checking-in with oneself and the class, and the capacity to then select the best teaching strategies toward the best goals, with thoughtful, insightful, and mindful skill. This combination does not lessen the fear or anxiety teachers face upon entering a classroom, but it helps teachers gain awareness of what they feel, the knowledge that the feeling will pass, and the ability to work while sitting with such feelings. As I progress in my identity as a "community-based, compassionate, embodied, contemplative teacher educator," my next step is to conduct analysis on the impacts of contemplative practices in Jesuit-trained teachers.

ESSENTIAL IDEAS TO CONSIDER

- Connecting community experiences with contemplative practices in teacher preparation programs allow preservice teachers to notice and work with their bodies, minds, and emotions.
- By paying attention to our thoughts, feelings, and bodies while teaching, we can shift our responses toward others from impulsive reactions to compassionate responses.
- When teacher educators model embodied emotions, preservice teachers increase their capacity for embodied presence.

REFERENCES

Bolte Taylor, J. (2009). *My stroke of insight: A brain scientist's personal journey.* New York, NY: Penguin Books.
Brach, T. (2012). *True refuge: Finding peace and freedom in your own awakened heart.* New York, NY: Bantam Books.

Brown, R. C. (2011). The mindful teacher as the foundation of contemplative pedagogy. In J. Simmer-Brown & F. Grace (Eds.), *Meditation and the classroom: Contemplative pedagogy for religious studies* (pp. 75–84). Albany, NY: State University of New York Press.

Castro, O., & Grassi, E. (2014). Finding the unfamiliar in familiar places: The Regis community-based Spanish/English exchange project: Journeys in place. In K. E. Eifler & T. M. Landy (Eds.), *Becoming beholders: Cultivating sacramental imagination and actions in college classrooms* (pp. 232–256). Collegeville, MI: Liturgical Press.

Grace, F. (2011). From content to context to contemplation: One professor's journey. In J. Simmer-Brown & F. Grace (Eds.), *Meditation and the classroom: Contemplative pedagogy for religious studies* (pp. 47–64). Albany, NY: State University of New York Press.

Grassi, E., & Castro, O. (2011). Learning from our neighbors: Teachers studying "abroad" with local immigrant families. *Accelerate Quarterly Review of the National Clearinghouse for English Language Acquisition, 4*(1), 10–12.

Grassi, E., & Armon, J. (2015a). Re-envisioning TESOL in teacher education: The transformative power of teachers studying "abroad" in the neighborhood. In J. M. Perren & A. J. Wurr (Eds.), *Learning the language of global citizenship: Strengthening service-learning in TESOL* (pp. 420–459). Champaign, IL: Common Ground Publishers.

Grassi, E., & Armon, J. (2015b). Re-envisioning teacher education: The transformative power of teachers studying "abroad" in the neighborhood. In A. S. Tinkler, B. E. Tinkler, V. M. Jagla, & J. R. Strait (Eds.), *Service-learning to advance social justice in a time of radical inequality* (pp. 189–221). Charlotte, NC: Information Age Publishing.

Hanson, R. (2013). *Hardwiring happiness: The new brain science of contentment, calm, and confidence.* New York, NY: Harmony Books.

Jennings, P. A. (2015). *Mindfulness for teachers: Simple skills for peace and productivity in the classroom.* New York, NY: W.W. Norton.

Salzberg, S. (2014). *Real happiness at work: Meditations for accomplishment, achievement, and peace.* New York, NY: Workman Publishing.

Index

About the Editors and Contributors

Jane E. Dalton, Ph.D., is an assistant professor of art education at the University of North Carolina at Charlotte, teaching art education and studio art. Her research interests include contemplative pedagogy and social-emotional learning in classrooms using the arts. Jane's work as a textile artist has been exhibited throughout the United States. She is the coauthor of *The Compassionate Classroom: Lessons that Nurture Empathy and Wisdom* (2004).

Elizabeth Hope Dorman, Ph.D., is associate professor of teacher education at Fort Lewis College, a public liberal arts college in Durango, Colorado, where she teaches graduate and undergraduate students in secondary, K–12, elementary education, and teacher leadership programs. Her scholarship focuses on the integration and effects of mindfulness and contemplative pedagogies on teacher development of social-emotional competence, particularly in diverse contexts and courses that address multicultural perspectives and equity issues.

Kathryn Byrnes , Ph.D., is the Baldwin Program Director in the Center for Learning and Teaching at Bowdoin College in Brunswick, Maine, and faculty at the Teachings in Mindful Education (TiME) Institute in Maine. She served as board president of the Mindfulness in Education Network (MiEN), and taught in-person and online courses on mindful education at Lesley University in Cambridge, Massachusetts, and at Bowdoin College. Her scholarship and professional development work focuses on the integration of contemplative pedagogy in educational contexts.

* * *

Heather Bair is a transpersonal psychotherapist in private practice working with children, families, and the LGBT population. Heather utilizes mindfulness, movement, art, and play with clients

Deborah Donahue-Keegan is a lecturer in the Department of Education at Tufts University. Since participating in the CARE for Teachers intensive retreat, she has been integrating mindfulness into her courses. Deborah is also the cofounder and codirector of the Massachusetts Consortium for Social-Emotional Learning in Teacher Education.

Katinka Gøtzsche has a master of arts in psychology and dramaturgy from Aarhus University, Denmark. She is a teacher in Silkeborg Gymnasium, an upper secondary school in Denmark. Besides working as a teacher, she also works as a coach for students with personal and school-related problems and teaches courses and seminars on empathy and presence led by the Danish Society for the Promotion of Life Wisdom in Children.

Elizabeth Grassi is a professor of linguistically and culturally diverse education and director of faculty assessment. Elizabeth was a K–12 teacher and coordinator of culturally and linguistically diverse language acquisition programs in the United States and abroad.

Tim Jester is an associate professor in the College of Education at the University of Alaska Anchorage. He is faculty in the elementary education preservice program and coordinator of the M.Ed. in teaching and learning. His scholarship focuses on teacher education that aims to support educators' development of intercultural competence and skills in culturally responsive teaching through cross-cultural field experiences and reflective practices.

David Lee Keiser is an associate professor in the Department of Secondary and Special Education at Montclair State University. He writes about contemplative pedagogy and Eastern perspectives on education. A recent publication, "Buddhas Still in Classrooms: Where Is the Mustard Seed?" appeared in *Reflective Practice* (2015).

Jambay Lhamo is a lecturer in Paro College of Education, Royal University of Bhutan. Her research interests include mindfulness practice in her personal and professional life. She is also interested in promoting the study of compassionate classroom pedagogy.

Matt Spurlin is a Ph.D. candidate at the University of Denver. His dissertation is on curricular agency and the contemplative development of curriculum. He currently teaches educational philosophy at the University of Northern Colorado.